still.
groovin'

still groovin'

affirmations for women in the second half of life

ruth beckford

SOURCEBOOKS, INC.®
NAPERVILLE, ILLINOIS

Published by Sourcebooks
P.O. Box 4410, Naperville, Illinois 60567-4410
(630) 961-3900
FAX: 630-961-2168

First edition published 1999 by The Pilgrim Press. Paperback edition published 2000 by Sourcebooks, Inc., by arrangement with The Pilgrim Press.

Library of Congress Cataloging-in-Publication Data
Beckford, Ruth.
Still groovin' : affirmations for women in the second half of life / Ruth Beckford.
    p. cm.
Originally published: Cleveland, OH : Pilgrim Press, 1999.
ISBN 1-57071-529-7 (alk. paper)
  1. Middle aged women–Psychology. 2. Middle aged women–Attitudes. 3. Aging–Psychological aspects. 4. Self-actualization (Psychology) I. Title.

HQ1059.4 .B44 2000
305.244–dc21   00-024642

Printed and bound in the United States of America

DR   10   9   8   7   6   5   4   3   2   1

still groovin'

Ruth Beckford

Still groovin'? How can that be?
You thought groovin' ended around forty-three.
At least, that's what the media wanted you to think—
that good times and good looks ended in a blink.

Forty-three candles spelled the sure fate of doom
'cause in the world of glamour and sex
there was no room
for women in the second half of life;
their days should be filled with gloom and strife.

Nonsense! Not true, I say,
forty-three candles just light your way
up the path of wisdom and confidence
no longer on that indecision fence.
Taking sure, honest steps of maturity,
say it out loud, "I love being me."

Contents

Preface

This book has been a lifetime in the making. As a baby in the crib, I moved to the beat, and as soon as I was able to walk, I danced. I just loved to move. Private lessons began when I was three years old, back in 1928. I was the first and only black student at Florelle Batsford's studio in downtown Oakland, California, and I studied all forms of dance, from tap to classical ballet. By eight years of age, I was a paid vaudeville performer. By my teen years, I was well into my career—dancing, giving solo concerts, and winning many competitions. At seventeen, I toured professionally with the famous Katherine Dunham Company, perfecting her unique style of African Caribbean dance. During that time I also continued my studies as the first and only black modern dance student at the University of California at Berkeley and at the Anna Halprin/Welland Lathrop Modern Dance Studio in San Francisco, later becoming a member of the company.

In 1947, I founded a city–funded recreational modern dance program in Oakland—the first in the nation. My goal was to help young girls develop self-esteem through the art and discipline of dance. I taught classes and ran the program until 1967. In 1953, I opened the first African American Haitian dance studio in Oakland, and later opened one in San Francisco as well. My dance company's closing concert was at Cal–Berkeley in 1961. I closed both studios in 1975, ending my career in dance. I felt I had achieved my goals, and I believe it's wise to close a career while it is still fun and at a high peak.

Some women would have said that two careers are enough. But I could not sit still. I started acting in the early 1970s at the Oakland Ensemble Theatre and studied with its founder, Ron Stacker Thompson. He and I cowrote 'Tis the Morning of My Life, an older woman—younger man romantic comedy that I produced and starred in. We sold out and were a hit. We went on to write two sequels, both meeting with the same success. In 1989, the original cast went to New York, off Broadway, and was a hit again. I have continued acting on television and in films.

Today I am a busy senior. I study stained-glass cutting and mentor a young teenage girl. One day a week I work for the Private Industry Council as a life skills counselor and motivator for men and women in preapprentice nontraditional trades. A few have met with drugs, poverty, and just plain bad luck. In each case, I have attempted to help them regain their confidence and self-esteem. Many of my students have stayed in touch with me.

Still Groovin' has emerged from these life experiences. I have tried to include both humorous and serious affirmations for women who are forty-five and older—what I am calling the second half of life. I have found—and I hope you will also—that this half of life is even more rewarding and fulfilling than the first half.

Acknowledgments

Thanks, and my love, to these extraordinary folks:

To Mama and Daddy, my guardian angels perched on my shoulders, for surrounding me with a "You can do it," supportive, safe, love-filled foundation. To my sister, Roselyn, and my late twin brothers, Fowler and Felix, for always being in my corner.

To Ron and Cle Thompson, Maya Angelou, and Danny Glover, for their loyalty and longtime, family-like friendships.

To Brenda Mabry, Dr. Dorothy Patterson, Dr. Julia Hare, and Dr. Ruth Love, whom I lovingly call my scholarly sister-friends, for listening with kind hearts.

To Alfre Woodard, my newfound friend, for her talent and generous professionalism, and for her warmth and patience with me on the set of *Funny Valentine*. Alfre is a true role model for today's young mothers.

To Donna Williams, my personal editor and friend, for smoothing out the edges and hanging in there.

To Sheryl Fullerton, my agent, who believed in *Groovin'* and in me, for going the extra mile and making sure it got published.

To my baby boomer play daughters, Deborah Vaughn, Elendar Barnes, Shirley Brown, Naima Lewis, Mildred Howard, Mary Vivian, Margarette Robinson, and Albirda Rose, and my niece, Linda Speed.

To the Pilgrim Press staff: Timothy Staveteig, for selecting *Still Groovin'* to be published, and for his positive support throughout the process; Martha Clark, for the beautiful, creative design; Nathan Bubenzer, for seeing to it that everyone knows about *Groovin'*; and Ed Huddleston, for the finishing touches and for holding my hand through my impatience.

Part One

Health

groovin'

1   I will get a free face-lift by smiling.

2   I will take time to pamper myself.

3   Life moves at its own pace.

4   I've been healed before.

5   I will go easy on myself.

6   Like the redwood tree, I grow more beautiful with age.

7   I am always just fine, thank you.

8   I see myself as strong.

9   I didn't complain today, not even once.

10 When I wake up feeling blah, I dress in my favorite outfit.

11 I am a survivor; I have been to the mountaintop and back.

12 I feel good when I volunteer.

13 From my head to my feet, I am alive and well.

14 Before I get up, I will give myself a good stretch.

15 I am energized by God.

16 I will become a more creative cook.

17 I will swallow my pride again and get my annual mammogram.

18 My feet are my foundation, the link to my good health.

19 I will not let the fear of embarrassment keep me at home.

20 I will not let vanity get in the way of my hearing.

21 I know medication will not heal without meditation.

22 I make plans for Medicare—even if it's twenty years away.

23 I will stay independent as long as it's safe and possible.

24 A hug is a gourmet meal to my skin.

25 I will give the gift of life as long as I can.

26 When it comes to food, don't sweat the small stuff.

27 My arms are too short.

28 Whew! Did someone turn on the heater?

29 Who changed the mirrors in my room?

An ache here, a pain there. So what?

Health is your most valuable possession, and it's priceless. Poor folks can be rich in health, and millionaires can be paupers. If you are in your forties, then you can lock in the richness of health right now. If your golden years have been increasingly beset by illness, then know that you can gain control of your "health wealth" today—regardless of what the doctors and researchers report.

For example, we hear that with each passing year, our cells reproduce more slowly. This means that the healing process takes longer. But I ask you, who's racing the clock? I'm not concerned if it'll take four days or four weeks longer than when I was twenty. The important thing is that I will heal. Better yet, sickness does not automatically have to kick in when you turn forty-five or fifty-five or sixty-five. As long as you have breath, you can begin to take control of your body.

For more than forty years, you've been told what to do: eat balanced, low-fat meals with lots of roughage; don't smoke; go easy on the alcohol; exercise often. Walking is great. Get regular checkups. We know all the rules. But let's face it, habit and lack of discipline are the enemies to quality healthy living.

We can use that knowledge beginning today. Having to tote a sack of medicine on an all-day outing may not be fun, but the instruction to "take the pink pill every four hours" means every four hours. Weather reports have new and deeper meanings after age forty-five. A change in weather can cause joint aches. Cold, damp days don't mix with arthritis, so what is a woman in her second half of life to do? Well, you can crawl back under the covers and wait for the storm to pass. Or you can go slower today. What's the rush?

People fear the second half of life because they think that sickness and body breakdown are givens. They aren't! Good health is possible for the entirety of your life. Our wonderful bodies were not designed to break down until well after one hundred years of age; God didn't build in planned obsolescence. Your body was designed to hold up under incredible stresses. That does not mean, however, that you can maintain the wild and crazy lifestyle of a twenty-year-old. (Even twenty-year-olds shouldn't attempt such lifestyles.) You can't party all night and still expect to be alert the next day. If you are still young and do not believe me, then try it. But be honest with yourself the next day. See how tired and sluggish you will be. Nor can you eat everything as you once did. Be vigilant about what goes into your mouth. Love yourself. Be good to your body.

Be just as vigilant about what goes into your mind. Poisonous thoughts poison bodies. Let go of "stuff." Let go of old grudges. Let go of anger. Let go of chronic worries. Say to yourself, "Today I will think only uplifting thoughts." Do it until it becomes a good habit. Remember, you can choose to be happy, or you can choose to be sad. It's up to you.

Having good health also means staying safe. Women over forty-five, especially seniors, are often targeted by muggers and con artists. But you don't have to be helpless. You can still be in control when you change some old habits. For example, park in well-lighted areas, walking quickly to your car when you are out at night. Be alert to your surroundings and other people. Have your key in your hand before you reach your car. If you are apprehensive, then go directly to a parking attendant or a nearby store. I love going to the movies alone, but I don't go at night anymore. It's too dangerous. I now go to matinees. For evening events, I call a friend. Seniors should avoid solitary night outings.

Living alone in the old family home may no longer be wise. Neighborhoods change, and your support system may no longer be there. You could be vulnerable for a home invasion. For younger women just in the second half of life, a sophisticated alarm system may stop the anxiety. But many find that a secure condominium or apartment is even friendlier. Consider moving to a senior complex. It's wonderful having a manager who must be responsible for that leaky faucet and roof repairs. Lonely? Bored? Many complexes provide planned recreational activities.

Your health is indeed your wealth. Read over the following reflections and affirmations, and begin to take control of your body's health. It all starts in the mind.

1

I will get a free face-lift by smiling.

"Can this be me I see in the mirror? It can't be!" At forty-five, I was in shock. I actually had a line at the corner of each eye. I ran to a better light. It had to be a shadow, right? Wrong. There it was, clear as day. A line. I wasn't ready to call it a wrinkle. I decided to save that word until I was at least fifty. As time went by and fifty became history, I looked in the mirror again. My face was a mass of wrinkles and folds. When I shifted positions, some of the wrinkles and folds disappeared, thank goodness. I decided it was a gravity thing. If you don't believe me, just hold a mirror and bend over. Brace yourself. Now look.

You can call them smile lines, wisdom lines, or signs of aging gracefully, but the truth is, they are wrinkles. Plain old wrinkles. How can any of those wrinkle creams with sophisticated names (you know—the ones with expensive-looking labels) work? If they did, would there be one wrinkled woman on earth? I once took a trip to a plastic surgeon to price out a more aggressive wrinkle strategy. The shock of a $10,000 bill to restore my face helped me decide that a trip to the Caribbean was a better use for my money—and I could make more than one trip.

There is a natural, healthy way to minimize the appearance of wrinkles. Just look in the mirror and consciously let every muscle relax, droop. Then slowly lift your brows. Open your eyes slightly wider than usual, feel the muscles lift, and now...smile.

A smile softens my wrinkles because it lifts my disposition. I will get a free face-lift today by smiling—and smiling often.

I will take time to pamper myself.

Rush, rush, rush. When you were younger and single, it seemed as if you never had the time to make a well-balanced meal because there was always a test to cram for, a party to go to, or a date to go out on. Many women marry and have children, or they have aging parents who need increasing amounts of care. Either way, your focus became much more domestic—and service oriented. You were on call for everybody's needs except your own. Besides being the neighborhood pied piper, you were the short-order cook, the maid, the doctor, the lover, and the accountant. It's a wonder you had any energy left to crawl into bed at night.

For women early in the second half of life, arrange to have an evening away from after-school activities. Perhaps you can drive a car pool every other week so that you can take in an elegant quiet time. Or once each week at lunch, take your sandwich with you to a park or purchase a salad at a deli.

For other women, the kids are grown up, the nest is empty, and now is the perfect time to begin learning how to be good to yourself. Maybe you're cooking for one now, maybe two. If you can afford it, occasionally buy more expensive food items. Set a glamorous table. Use your best china and silver. Light a candle. Sip your wine or soda out of your best stemware. It's good not to have to rush, rush, rush.

Even when eating alone, I can dine in gracious company.

3

Life moves at its own pace

"Patience, patience," I kept telling myself. The shoe clerk must have taken slow-motion pills. She walked with the oozing speed of thick molasses. She sauntered to the stockroom and sauntered back, only to say that they didn't have my size. She even talked slowly. I had to reflect on what patience really meant.

Pause. Take time out from your hectic day. Accent only the activities that you thoroughly enjoy. Impatience stems from doing too much stuff that you have to do rather than love to do.

Count to ten when you feel impatience creeping in. Inhale deeply. Being uptight makes for shallow breathing. Overreacting to tension causes stress-related illnesses.

For women just in the second half of life, you may still be attending soccer games or encouraging a ballet student. While your charges are attending to their activities, take a brisk walk around the field or block. Use the time wisely to become healthier and fit.

All women should exercise three to five times a week or anytime that situations become too tense. Never shout, scream, or treat others badly. Just because you're in a rush doesn't give you the right to misbehave. Clear your list of people who are no longer worthy of your time. Unload negative baggage. Become patience personified.

Life moves at its own pace. Practicing patience keeps me in tune with my life and hopes.

4

I've been healed before.

When I was a child, I bumped my head on the cabinet door. I watched the knob swell up, and it hurt. Mama kissed it and then put an ice pack on it. Because I was an active, uninhibited girl, the accidents became more frequent—and intense. Sometimes I'd need stitches for cuts or casts for broken bones.

After forty-five, there are more reasons to be cautious. Bones become less dense with age, and we heal more slowly. While golf, tennis, swimming, and power walking are all relatively safe, our equilibrium sometimes is a bit off. For seniors, falls are all too common. Other problems can come without warning. One day you're okay, the next the doctor is saying "We need to talk."

I heard those very same words two years ago. I knew what the doctor was going to say. My mind cried out, Not another surgery. I can't go through the pain and long rehabilitation again. He believed the surgery would improve my condition, a pinched spinal cord. It had to. I could hardly walk, even with a walker. My previous surgeries had successfully corrected some lower back problems. This was to be my first thoracic, just above the waist. After I finished crying and feeling sorry for myself, I said, "Let's get the show on the road as soon as possible. I'm ready for my grand opening." So in March 1997, I had my fifth back surgery. Today, I'm walking much better, and I'm careful not to overdo it.

Your history has proved that your body can heal itself. Have faith in your body and in your doctor, and you can cope with any maladies.

I am a survivor. I've been healed before, and I am healed again. I listen to my body because it speaks to my needs and because it affirms me. My body knows what is best.

I will go easy on myself.

Think back to younger days. Companies loved to hire us because we put in that extra effort. We worked hard to make our companies, homes, and churches operate efficiently—often to our own discomfort. We smiled through the pain. We went to work on days when we should have stayed in bed.

Yet even with our extra effort, there are still nagging doubts about our abilities as we grow older. Can we still cut it? Can we still carry our share of the load? Of course we can. We may not be able to do the fifty-yard dash in ten seconds (could we ever do that?), but we can do most things we used to do. If we move at a slightly slower pace, so what!

I remember overdoing my first time on a stair-climbing exerciser. The next morning I could hardly move. Thank goodness for the elevator.

Our wisdom and years of experience more than compensate for the slowing down. Younger folks appreciate us, too. They often seek advice from their older coworkers on anything from getting promoted to coping with personal relationships to buying a dream house. We have been there. We have experience more valuable than misguided energy.

I will pace myself. If I feel stiff, I'll take the elevator or sit down until I feel better. I am confident in my strengths, and I go easy on my limitations.

6

*Like the redwood tree,
I grow more beautiful with age.*

For most of our lives, we are consumed with outward appearances. We agonized over acne and zits during our teen years. Now we worry about wrinkles and sagging.

Sometime during our late thirties or early forties, we pulled out the first gray hair. Now that we are in the second half of life, we have given up pulling out such hairs because they all seem poised to turn gray.

The battle of the bulge has proved rather constant. But as we grow older, our motivation to lose weight seems to lessen, and our willingness to accept a roll here or sag there increases. Earlier we were concerned with wearing a string bikini, but now we would be pleased to look good in a one-piece suit.

As our bodies begin to sag with age, we put more energy into improving our inner health. We are less uptight, and an aura of calm is reflected in our eyes.

Like the redwood tree, I grow more beautiful with age. My bark may be thick and grooved, but my core is strong. I am more secure with my life and project an inner peace and strength that are the gifts of time.

I am always just fine, thank you.

"How are you?" "Fine, and yourself?" How many years have you said "Fine" when things weren't fine? It's an automatic exchange, the way we greet each other. He may not have listened for a response because he has other things on his mind, or she may not really care how you feel. Perhaps we are afraid that the other person may become impatient if we list all the aches and concerns that we truly feel.

Doctors and dentists, however, need to hear truthful responses to the question, "How do you feel?" But maybe they seem impatient when you make a list. Insist that they listen; after all, you pay for their services. Some doctors see gray hair and dismiss all ailments as a normal part of the aging process. Not true. Divine life is always within you. Your magnificent body is always renewing itself.

So if you don't feel good, find out why. It's not always aging. As you get older, make sure that you also know all about your medications. What are their potential side effects? Between appointments, write down questions you want answered, and read them off to your physician at the next visit. Physicians' assistants, nurses, and others can also be helpful.

Don't let visiting the dentist frighten you, either. There are so many new things nowadays to alleviate pain that it's a breeze. There's no need to lose perfectly good teeth to gum disease. Keep those gums firm. Use a toothpaste for sensitive teeth, and floss every day or use a Water Pic.

If it is necessary to have teeth extracted, be sure to have the dentist duplicate the look and color of your originals as nearly as possible. False teeth today are great impostors. Only your dentist knows for sure.

I will keep a healthy mind in a healthy body so that I can remain as natural as in my youth.

You can feel unwell at any age—this feeling is not reserved for the back fifties. But when you're still in the early part of the second half of life—from forty-five to fifty-five—become aware of your body. You've been with it long enough to know when you are off your mark. But oftentimes women ignore bodily signs because they're too busy. Have you already told yourself that? Next time listen to your body.

When you don't feel well, even when it's a minor illness, your morale can falter. A head cold can make you feel down. If one area of the body weakens, then I think the remainder of the body acts as a support system. You must be patient with your healing because your body has less energy. You do not have a button to push and get better.

Like many dancers, I have needed additional repairs to my body. I remember lying in the hospital in 1981 after my low-back spinal fusion. I was in great pain and full of self-pity. The nurse had just gotten me back into bed from my first attempt at walking after surgery. I hurt all over. Tears were streaming down my cheeks; the pain medication hadn't kicked in yet.

It hadn't occurred to me that I could have lost the use of my legs. I heard groans coming from the room next to mine. I said to my nurse, "I guess someone else just had back surgery too." "No," said the nurse, "that's a young man who just had both legs amputated, the result of a bad motorcycle accident." I stopped feeling sorry for myself and said a prayer for him.

I rejoice that my inner power is healing me minute by minute, day by day.

I didn't complain today, not even once.

Do you know someone who is a habitual complainer? As we enter the second half of life, we grumble about our parents and kids; we gripe about bosses and stress. Everything seems a major interruption. We could push against punches, but it's much easier to roll with them—and lessen their impact. The best way to roll with life's inconveniences is to avoid the habit of complaining.

People who complain as they enter the second half of life tend to complain even more as they grow older. Think about the complaints you have heard in the past month. The biggest source of complaints is health. Hot flashes are ruining this person's life. The doctor doesn't give that person enough time. The medication makes this person sick and is too expensive for that one. His glasses don't fit anymore. She gets out of breath going up stairs. And so on. How long do you enjoy listening to these complaints? Perhaps you sometimes wonder, "Why doesn't she keep them to herself? No one wants to hear all that stuff." And that's the point.

I have a friend who has a talent for describing her ailments. She makes her pains so graphic, you almost feel them. "The pain starts on each side of my head, just behind the ears, and then travels over to the top of my head in a pulsating beat. Then when the pain meets on the top, it explodes and shatters pain down the front of my forehead and down the back of my head to my neck."

That's her description of what you and I would classify as, "Yeah, I have a headache." But wait. Stop and smile to yourself, listen to your own words, and you will hear your complaint about her complaining.

I give myself a pat on my back. I didn't complain even once today.

When I wake up feeling blah,
I dress in my favorite outfit.

Yes, even wonderful you can have a blah day. On a blah day you wake up, but don't want to get up. Nothing hurts. You just feel blah. No headache, no stomachache—just blah. You can't even come up with an excuse for it. But it is a real feeling.

You know you can't give in to the blahs because you have things to do. Lie there a little longer and decide what your favorite outfit is. It may be a little dressier than what you usually wear, but as long as it isn't sequins and lace, be a little dressy today. Now you are ready to venture out of bed.

Wear your sensible heels with an adequate toe width and comfort for your feet. Take your time dressing and putting on your makeup. Imagine that you're going to meet that person you've always admired from afar—man or woman. You've appreciated the person's strength, and it has often motivated you. You reach your destination, and everyone compliments you on how good you look. Sincere compliments always boost your morale.

Someone asks, "What's the occasion?" And you reply with an affirmation: Today I'm giving myself the gift of being the best me I can be.

11

I am a survivor; I have been to the mountaintop and back.

I was so frightened I couldn't catch my breath. My skin was cold and hot at the same time. I got a funny taste in my mouth. I thought my ears had played a trick on me. The doctor couldn't be saying what I thought I heard.

But it was true. The tests all proved it. I was ill, seriously ill. I had a blood clot in my lungs. This, on the fourth day following my fifth back surgery. Now what? After the uncontrollable tears, I settled down. I had to because my lungs hurt even more when I cried.

The doctor was patient with me, telling me the facts as I had requested. I needed time to be alone to think, but there wasn't time. I had to get to the radiation lab to pinpoint the extent of the clot and get on an IV immediately. I was in the hospital for four days having my blood thinned. For the following six months, I was on a controlled diet and medication.

As a dancer, I'm used to being injured. But being so sick with a life-threatening illness was new to me. I turned my newfound problem over to God. Only God could give me the strength to face the future months of healing.

I know that God will help my every need and bring me through.

I feel good when I volunteer.

During your late forties and early fifties, you never seem to find the time to do any volunteer work. But you need to find such time. Involve yourself as a volunteer at your children's school. Chaperone events. You don't have to be a regular volunteer who is scheduled to be at a certain place at a certain time each week. Just volunteer when you can manage. It takes planning. It's just another bonding opportunity with your children or teens.

If your children are grown and gone, you probably can better find the time to volunteer. You will get so much joy out of it that you might feel guilty. Volunteering is keeping you mentally healthy.

I volunteer two times a week for two completely different programs, one day with a public information project and one day with teen girls. I have to plan what to wear, and that gets me out of my sweats and into casual clothes. I pull it all together so that my appearance is pleasant. Not only should I look good, but I must be in good spirits so that the people I touch are uplifted, too. Keeping a smile on my face keeps me positive.

Volunteering keeps me emotionally alert and motivated. I stay upbeat, and I enjoy being in touch with people.

13

From my head to my feet,
I am alive and well.

"Thank you, God," should be our chant several times a day. We always need to cherish this miracle machine—the body. And this mantra needs to increase as we ease into our fifties.

Take some time to think about what your body does second by second without any conscious effort on your part. It will astound you. Not just the big, obvious organs such as heart, lungs, and liver, but your digestive system, eyes, brain, ears—all doing their own thing nonstop.

Yet you hardly give all these complicated functions a single thought until one of them ceases to work. Then you run to the doctor. Her diagnosis might frighten you enough to change for a while, but then you're back to your old bad habits of indifference. And this can lead to ignoring bodily signs and avoiding healthy steps such as rest, eating well, and exercising.

Stop right now and proclaim a new attitude: "From this day forward, I resolve to make proper care of my body a high priority in my daily routine."

One of the things I do every morning, as soon as my feet hit the floor, is go to the kitchen, fill my plastic quart bottle to the top with water, and drink all of it before I leave the sink. I know the value of water in the body, and it's a free contributor to good health. So, why not? I found that if I use a straw, it's much easier to get the quart down. Adding a slice of an orange or lemon can also help. Then during the rest of the day I can easily sip a second quart.

I love my body and pledge to take good care of it every day.

Before I get up, I will give myself a good stretch.

While you are still in your forties, get into the habit of addressing your body with respect. Good posture should be a habit by now. If it isn't, then start today to discipline yourself so that your spine is in alignment.

You can save yourself a lot of grief if you pay attention to your posture. It's easy to slump in your chair or stand with your shoulders rounded because as you age, your muscle mass changes. Posture relates directly to your health because you need all of your lung capacity to breathe properly. And you get that when you stand upright. Slumping in a chair curves your spine and puts pressure on your hip joints.

To keep good circulation, you should stretch your body as far as you can while you are still in bed, as though you were a taut rubber band. Hold the position a few seconds, and then relax. Do this several times. Along with your stretch, fill your lungs and push your breath all the way out on the release.

I breathe deep and stretch, and I feel great.

15

I am energized by God.

In your early fifties, your energy can decrease with each year—if you let it. There's a rhythm of movement that says, "Look at me. I'm young." But later it becomes, "Look at me. I'm still here!" You must not let yourself be cast in the role of slow mover because that's what everyone thinks the later years are about. Says who?

Most folks move slowly not because of a disability but because of their attitude. Move with a purpose, even if you have no particular purpose to fulfill.

When you stand up, leave the chair as if you have something important to do. Move with a light step in comfortable shoes. High heels won't work as well. There are plenty of attractive low-heel styles, so don't torture yourself with old habits.

I move with a purpose and an upbeat attitude. I'm in possession of God's energy.

I will become a more creative cook.

Your doctor wants you on a fat-free—well, reduced fat—diet. "He expects me to change the cooking habits of my whole life? I don't want to learn any newfangled ways of cooking. Besides, low-fat food just doesn't taste good."

Many people in our time-crunched world have two menu ideas: home-delivered pizza or Chinese takeout. We don't think we have time to plan tasty, healthy, and satisfying meals. For a woman who has just entered the second half of life, you may be working more than eight hours each day (yes, working at home on the weekends as well). You're juggling work and family responsibilities. For a woman like me who has been in the second half a while, you may not want to spend all the time and energy needed to cook for one.

Your food choices are an important factor in good health. Find a time each week to jot down dinner ideas for the next week. Do this before you make your shopping list. Build a pantry stocked with wholesome foods that are quick to boil or bake or microwave. Low-fat food doesn't have to taste bad. In fact, I've found the secret of good taste in cooking with herbs, spices, and garlic. Experiment with a new book of recipes. I promise you that a baked chili chicken beats a more traditional (and plain) salted-and-peppered chicken every time. Also add more vegetables, beans, and grains to your diet.

I am satisfied with my life and body because I am eating in a healthy way.

17

I will swallow my pride again and get my annual mammogram.

Ugh! How I hate my annual mammogram. I call my HMO several weeks in advance to set up an appointment, then I start the process of convincing myself the actual exam isn't all that bad. Yeah, right. I remind myself that the cold tray they place my anatomy on isn't freezing cold. They send people to outer space. Why can't they have some sort of thermal material lining the tray?

When I arrive at the doctor's office, I save myself the embarrassment of having the nurse say, "Oops, looks like we need a larger slate." Right away I volunteer that I need the biggest one. "Take a deep breath now. Hold still." I take a deep breath and hold still. Click. "Now breathe." I breathe. After several clicks she tells me to get dressed and adds that I will be getting a card of clearance in the mail in a few days.

And I do get a card several days later. Everything is fine. Thank you, God. And even though I hate to do it, it's the intelligent way to be in control of my blessed body. My card did say I was fine. Whew! Peace of mind for another year.

I get my annual mammogram because I know the value of early detection.

My feet are my foundation, the link to my good health.

I will begin to respect my feet. They've been the under-dog long enough.

When you were born, someone may have placed your footprint on your birth certificate. Your parents often kissed the bottom of your feet, and each toe is a little piggy, the nursery rhyme tells us. Then during your adult-hood, either you or a pedicurist kept your toenails groomed and polished. All the while, your feet protested only when you insisted on going barefoot on a too-hot sandy beach or you foolishly followed fashion and squeezed them into pointed-toe, spike-heeled shoes.

As we get older, though, we can draw on some com-mon sense. We can find comfortable but style-conscious shoes now. Designers have learned to conform. There are fashionable low- and mid-heel shoes that don't overlap your toes into a point or look like orthopedic shoes. Now when your nails need cutting, you may visit the podiatrist as well as the pedicurist, especially since it's not so easy to reach your feet anymore. You don't need that nail polish. You just need good, short, healthy nails. And remember, if you have diabetes, never cut your own.

I treat my feet like the key to health and comfort that they are. Dancers' feet are jokingly called "shoes" because they are often callused and misshapen. Thank goodness, my feet don't conform to the rule; I have soft feet. Ballet dancers often get bunions. Because "the show must go on," dancers are known to perform on blisters and split–open calluses.

You must go on as well. And to do this with style, baby your feet.

I'll prop up my feet and soak them on occasion because they carry me all day.

I will not let the fear of embarrassment keep me at home.

The biggest source of embarrassment for women is almost a no-no to discuss—incontinence, commonly called weak bladder (although it's really the muscle that's weak). This condition can affect women throughout the second half of life. This weakness can cause leaking or urination to be uncontrollable.

Certainly it's embarrassing to wet yourself while you're awake. You ask yourself if you're in a second childhood when you awaken to a wet bed. You're reluctant to speak to your doctor about it. What would she or he think? You can increasingly become housebound because you don't want to have an accident in public.

Not to address this condition, or any of the other changes we face, can make our world smaller and smaller. What keeps us from purchasing a pack of incontinence pads? Embarrassment at the checkout stand? Visualize it: you're on the way home with the package clutched under your arm. You couldn't wait to put it on. It fit perfectly. It didn't even show when you tested it under your pants or tight skirt.

Absorbent pads are only one remedy. See your gynecologist for physical ways to strengthen muscles. There are exercises to remedy this weakness. But the same holds true for any embarrassing condition that could keep us homebound.

I will address whatever fear or embarrassment threatens to shrink my world.

20

I will not let vanity get in the way of my hearing.

Folks mumble more than they used to, and you are constantly asking for repeats during conversations. The phone doesn't ring as loudly. What is going on? Hearing often decreases during the fifties. Unfortunately, hearing has a low priority on the health scale. Most doctors don't even have the proper testing equipment at their clinics. If you need to get your hearing tested, you'll probably be referred to a specialist.

Wearing a hearing device still carries something of a stigma. Why? We get bifocal glasses or dental bridgework without hesitation. So what is the problem about hearing aids? They're inconspicuous, well sunken into the ear cavity, practically out of sight. Obtain that hearing aid, and give yourself the gift of hearing clearly once again so that your friends can stop shouting.

I have a friend who needed hearing assistance and kept putting off getting help. I told her to order the amplified phone system because it would be more comfortable for her and her friends. Even movie theaters have audio enhancements for their patrons. Now we can converse with a normal volume and can understand each other. Thank goodness for technology.

I will embrace technology and abandon vanity to live a full, vibrant life.

I know medication will not heal without meditation.

Homemade medications, once called remedies, were always administered with love and determination. Your mother had to be determined to get that nasty medicine down your throat. Remember castor oil? You preferred the malady to that medicine. You prayed along with the medication, but it was a prayer to help you swallow it as fast as possible.

As a child, I feared getting a cold more than getting in trouble. Mama had a whole "cold production." She was a creative chemist and took her job seriously. In bed, I could hear her moving around downstairs in the kitchen, concocting her potion—the castor oil cocktail sandwich. I think she called it a sandwich because it was layered. First there was the juice of a lemon. Then the warmed castor oil went on top of that. Last was another layer of lemon juice. I then heard the fatal footsteps coming upstairs. As Mama got to my bed, she'd stir it all up and say, "Drink it while it's foaming." Oh, Lord, please help me! After I drank her cocktail, she had the nerve to give me a half lemon to suck on to cut the taste. I was an adult before I was able to drink lemonade without thinking about Mama's cocktail.

What are the home remedies that you grew up with? What prompted you to pray to get through it quickly? Focus on the connection. You know that the true healer is God. Meditation is as potent as the medication. Whenever I'm not feeling good, I take my medicine—and I have a quiet talk with God.

I meditate on the truth that I am God's child. I am healed.

22

I make plans for Medicare—
even if it's twenty years away.

In the "good old days" before Medicare, there was a program called Associated Charities—a 1930s federal program for the poor. But during that decade, who wasn't poor in material things? Associated Charities had clinics that gave free health care to families. I can remember the long lines that started early in the morning. Both the very ill and the not so ill had to wait their turn in the crowded hallways, everybody sharing germs.

Medicare, in contrast, gives superb medical care in the facility of your choice. Medicare doesn't take care of the total coverage. You need supplemental insurance, but an assortment of hospitals and insurance companies administer supplemental programs. So today, after age sixty-five, your medical needs are respectfully taken care of. I know that every time I go to one of my specialists, I'm receiving the best care. My A and B plans assure me coverage from low-cost prescriptions to major surgeries.

Peace is mine when I make plans for my medical coverage.

I will stay independent as long as it's safe and possible.

One day I was looking in the mirror, putting on my makeup, when I noticed that my face looked blurry. I kept wiping my bathroom mirror clean, but my face was still blurry. There were more problems: "I wish folks wouldn't drive with their bright lights turned on high," and "Oh, but the sun is bright today." Blurred vision and sensitivity to light are warning signs of cataracts. The eye doctor verified my suspicions. I wasn't too worried, because the surgery is done on an outpatient basis, and from my research, I found out it was painless. An added plus was the fact that cataract surgery has a high rate of success.

I still can't believe how easy it was. In during the morning, and out during the afternoon with an eye patch and several bottles of eye drops. The hourly drops were the biggest inconvenience. The next day, I drove myself to the exam. Wow! I could actually read the chart, no blurring. It was like a miracle. I had to wear my eye patch for a few weeks, and now I'm as good as new.

For those who are reluctant to have the surgery, you should stop driving. It's not an end to independence. You simply have to do more advance planning. Living alone may become scary if you're still in the big family home, and the everyday chores can be more troublesome.

Solutions: Have that surgery. Drive on surface streets, not the freeway. Eventually use cabs, public transportation, and/or senior shuttle service. Shop often so the load is lighter, and buy a little carry cart. Shop at off-peak hours. Clean on a regular basis only the rooms you use on a regular basis. Think about moving to a senior complex. Invest in sticky notes, and use them all over the house for reminders.

I won't sweat the little things so that I can stay as independent as possible.

A hug is a gourmet meal to my skin.

Research tells us that the offspring of wild animals will die if their mother doesn't lick, coddle, and play with them. Yes, even the mighty lioness must stroke her cubs, or they die. Have you ever watched how affectionate primates are? They can sit and groom each other for hours on end. It's the touching of each other that gives the contentment.

The skin is our biggest organ. It's just loaded with nerve endings to convey the sense of touch to us. Even the slightest breeze causes a reaction. Human babies have the same needs as wild animals. If they are never touched and held, they do not survive. If we adult humans do not continue to satisfy this need to be touched, we have what is referred to as "skin hunger."

Sometimes, as we age, we find ourselves alone. We become divorced or widowed. Children and friends move away. We must keep reaching out to new friends and be open to hugs.

Hugging assures my emotional well-being.

25

I will give the gift of life as long as I can.

If you are still in your forties, please consider being a bone marrow donor. It is a life-giving aid that only the young can give. It doesn't hurt, and it nourishes your spirit. How wonderful it would be if someone from every household gave a donation. This would also take care of the shortage of minority donors.

If you have moved into the second half of life, then you can still give the gift of life. "Are you feeling well?" That was the last question the nurse at the blood donor program asked me. It was the end of a long list of questions, but I didn't mind. I didn't even mind the needle because now they deaden the area of the big needle injection. Next they prick your finger to make sure your blood clots in the designated time. (Be sure they prick the side of your finger. It doesn't hurt as much later as pricking the fingerprint part.) Blood is badly needed, and you can safely give every two to three months. I specifically designate that my blood should go to the Children's Hospital Oakland Sickle Cell division.

I was falsely informed about being a blood donor. I had always heard that your blood wouldn't be taken if you were over sixty. Wrong information. As long as you're healthy, you can donate blood; it's bone marrow that has an age limit. So vow to do your part. Save a life. No excuses anymore.

Oh, and I almost forgot. This affirmation brings a bonus: you get all the coffee, juice, and cookies you want!

I will give the gift of life as long as I can; I will draw upon this gift as I need it.

When it comes to food, don't sweat the small stuff.

Food choices can bring out differences in women over forty-five. Some of my friends under fifty-five proclaim proudly, "I'm an organic eater. I eat only naturally grown products, no additives." I reply, "Whoop-de-do, good for you." Give me a break! It gets a little boring hearing them ask twenty questions of the waiter: "Are you sure this fish is grilled, not fried?" "Use only olive oil, please." "Have the chef hold the salt. I use only sea salt." Then they look at me and ask, "Are you going to eat that red meat?" "I sure am," I say and chomp down on a great rib eye steak or ham hock. While I'm enjoying my meal, they'll lecture me on the dangers of eating pork, not to mention chicken: "Is your chicken well done? E. coli, you know..."

They carry a small case full of vitamin supplements as a part of their health package. "If your food is so healthy, why is the sack of vitamins necessary?" I ask. "You can't be too fortified," they say. Then I have to endure the lecture on the value of mind-enhancing herbs and why I should drink red, not white, wine. Red, they say, is better for the heart.

Enough! My cholesterol is 105. My blood pressure is 120 over 80. I don't smoke, and I love an occasional good Bombay martini on the rocks. I hope that twenty-five years from now, they'll have the same clean bill of health that I do. So I shall continue to enjoy my sins. And if you are into natural foods and supplements, then congratulations. I will try to stay calm when I hear the words "organic," "natural," "fortified," and "no additives."

Let us agree: we are what we consume, so we will practice moderation.

27

My arms are too short.

I was in my late forties when I realized that the phone book was getting harder to read. No matter how far from my eyes I tried to hold it, the letters were still blurry. "The print's getting smaller," I said to no one in particular. Then I found myself using directory assistance more and more.

When things got too blurry, off I went to my eye doctor. He told me I needed reading glasses. I had a choice: if I didn't want to take them off and on, I could get bifocals with nonprescription upper lenses, or I could just have the entire lens for reading. Bifocals? He had to be kidding. I'm too young for bifocals. They're for old folks.

Well, after the shock wore off, I decided to get the sharpest pair of reading glasses I could find. I didn't mind taking them off and on. I was going down fighting. Bifocals? Not me.

I will get reading glasses and stop complaining of too short arms.

Whew! Did someone turn on the heater?

I have a friend who is extremely health conscious. You know the type: a vegetarian who drinks only bottled water, exercises regularly, and should take out stock in her favorite herbalist company. She reads books on the current holistic approach to all ailments and gives me unsolicited advice on how to live healthy and longer on herbs.

Entering the second half of life was a shock for her. She was fine until hot flashes became her constant companion. "Ms. Cool" in her thirties is now a "Red Hot Mama" in her late forties. I know it's not funny to her, but I can't help chuckling every time she breaks out in a sweat and exclaims, "Whew! Who turned on the heater?"

I have shared with her my one hot flash and how I conquered it. I ran, not walked, to my trusty gynecologist. Thank goodness for estrogen replacement therapy. I forgot I was going through menopause. I've pleaded my case to her to please respect her quality of life and see her gynecologist. She keeps loyal to the value of herbs to stop her flashes. Well, she's still flashing, and I'm still hiding my smiles.

For those of you going through the change of life, you may need to make some wardrobe and accessories adjustments. Wear panty hose only when necessary, and keep a jacket in the car for emergency "cold flashes."

Now my friend is complaining of sleep deprivation because of night sweats. I've been steadily brainwashing her with the joy of no flashes and sending her articles on replacement therapies. I hope that exhaustion and overall discomfort will help her to see the light. Still, it's her choice.

I will listen to my body and its needs as well as my friends' advice. But when transition comes, I will remain cool, calm, and collected; I will do what is best for me.

Who changed the mirrors in my room?

Little elves must have sneaked in during the midnight hours and replaced the mirrors in my room with carnival trick mirrors. "My goodness, everything is moving south." I'd always heard older women saying that, but I figured they just hadn't maintained exercise and proper diet. I never thought this dancer's body would turn on me. All those years of pliés and extensions, sore muscles and pulled tendons, to suddenly have the beginning of flabby thighs? "No, no, not me. It can't be. I'm only forty-seven."

I went in the bathroom to the full-length mirror, stripped down to my birthday suit, and took an inch-by-inch assessment. Oh, my goodness, it was true. Those tight thighs and butt were no longer "standing at attention." But, I thought, I'm not even fifty yet. What will happen then if I'm falling apart now?

I knew one thing for sure; I'd no longer wear just my favorite white leotard. No, it had to be accompanied by black tights at all times.

As my eyes traveled up, I breathed a sigh of relief. I still had a flat, firm stomach and small waist. Whew! My relief was short-lived. My body review indicated that it was time to move to the underwire bra. Even women with more compact breasts experience the "late forties body rebellion." (Give yourself this test. Lie flat on your back. Are your breasts now growing out of your sides? See what I mean?)

What to do? What to do? Do absolutely nothing. Be thankful that you still have a body that functions (even if you are missing a breast or have cottage cheese for thighs), and move on.

I will not fret over things moving south. I'll simply find a good seat and deal with the view.

Part Two

Empowerment

groovin'

30 I'm not the only one getting older—newborns are aging, too.

31 I'll never stop growing, regardless of my age.

32 I've earned the right to be outspoken, bold, vain, and selfish.

33 From this day forward I'll be honest about my feelings.

34 My knowledge puts me ahead of being threatened by youth.

35 I'll let go of things that I cannot change.

36 The early part of life got me ready for the adventure of the last part.

37 I'll celebrate honesty.

38 I'll give a sincere compliment to someone today.

39 My good thoughts will convert to good feelings and health.

40 I will celebrate birthdays with style.

41 I'll bury old guilts and nurture the seeds of self-esteem.

42 Now I have the courage to dig up secret ambitions and pursue them.

43 I'll listen to my inner voice and trusted friends a little more.

44 I no longer have the luxury of procrastination.

45 I'll pamper myself whenever I feel like it, even if it means eating beans for a week.

46 In the mirror I see both the problem and the solution.

47 I'll be as good to myself as I am to my best friend.

48 I won't take myself so seriously anymore.

49 I've been a dormant bud too long—it's my time to blossom.

50 I'll challenge myself to venture into a new, unfamiliar activity.

51 I'll go with the flowing stream because now it's my turn to float.

52 I can face disappointment because I know it's a temporary condition.

53 I decide which habits to retain or discard.

54 I am enthusiastic because enthusiasm has no age limit.

55 Now that I am alone, my plan is to live.

56 I'll take a big, bold step for a bold, new me.

57 I'll get my Ph.D. in rest.

58 Stress! Get over it already.

59 Tick tock, you can stop the clock.

Live as you jolly well please.

We seniors (and women just entering the second half of life can recall this time as well) were raised during an era that was, in many ways, kinder and gentler. We lived in real communities where we knew our neighbors, many of whom made up our extended family. We had play aunts, uncles, sisters, and cousins. We were taught as children to share and help one another. Women in particular were raised to be "nice" and service-oriented. While our mothers had us in the kitchen cooking, our brothers were outside playing and exploring.

Even though our lifestyle then was much more cooperative, the time also contained a shadow side, especially for women. We have all passed through women's liberation days, yet we knew deep down that the work at home still had to be done. Today we continue to shoulder much, if not all, of the household burden in addition to this new-found freedom of working outside the home.

That shadow side of our upbringing shows up in the fact that we still tend to neglect ourselves and our needs. The word "no" is nowhere to be found in many of our vocabularies. We were the Yes Generation, always anxious to please, ever in denial of personal needs and, in extreme cases, even willing to be walked on like the doormats too many of us were.

Live as you jolly well please? You may think this statement is the height of selfishness and insensitivity, but I'm here to tell you, there's no other way if you want to enjoy this mountaintop phase of your life.

It is time to serve yourself. Your life is to be enjoyed. Start now! Today. This instant. Stop being on demand. Learn to love taking time out for yourself. Work through the guilt; it'll pass. You'll be surprised how much time you'll have for yourself. Look at the amount of time you've spent serving everyone but yourself. Over the years you've been daughter, wife, mother, grandmother, cook, teacher, nurse, accountant, lover, janitor, doormat, and a whole lot more. Now it's your turn.

Have you ever wanted to do something really daring? Try wearing jeans and a sexy top to a formal after-five party. That'll wake up the old guy! Do it. Have you ever wanted to ride a motorcycle? Go for it! Go to a dealer, and tell the salesman you want him to take you for a test ride. Then climb on behind him and roarrr! Be adventurous. The most folks will say is that you've become eccentric in your later years. They wouldn't dare call you crazy, at least not to your face. Many will secretly envy your chutzpah. Read these affirmations over and over until you begin to believe that you too can become a part of life's exciting adventure.

I'm not the only one getting older— newborns are aging, too.

The United States has such a youth-oriented society, it makes me wonder if we've forgotten that everything and everyone on God's green earth ages. As far as I know, nothing moves in time from old age to newborn. Then why has it become such a crime to have wrinkles, grow gray hair, and slow down? Why are we trying to fight the accumulation of years? As a nation, we're in a terrible state of denial that's not only unhealthy, but also just plain foolish. If there is a Fountain of Youth, I'll probably be the first one to jump in, but until then, I'm going to enjoy my mountaintop years. I'm going to have a ball at every age.

Women are still lying about their age. Why? Now that companies can be sued over age discrimination, I see no reason to hide your arrival at a more sophisticated time in your life. The government is doing research in regard to moving the retirement age of sixty-five to seventy. We're living longer and healthier and looking better.

Some of my friends in their thirties were saying how much better they feel now than in their twenties. Someone else said, "Wait until your forties. That's when it's good." I had to smile and say, "It gets better with each decade." It's true. We are like fine wine.

I will celebrate what is best for me in each decade.

31

I'll never stop growing, regardless of my age.

Indigenous cultures around the world have rites of passage to mark the beginning of adulthood. In our country, however, laws tell us when we have reached that stage. It's a magic act. You reach eighteen (or in some states, twenty-one), and voilà! You're an adult. Suddenly you're expected to have self-confidence, calmness, intelligence, emotional control, and maturity enough to handle whatever life throws your way. Oh, really?

I never stop growing and learning. For example, new words and expressions are a constant challenge. You have to keep growing and learning just to be able to communicate. Remember how we went from ink pens to ballpoints? Waxed paper to foil and plastic? Milk bottles to milk cartons? Typing erasures to correction fluid to computer spell-checkers? I can still remember the thrill of slipping into my first pair of nylons and discarding my rayons. How about the shift from manual transmission as standard and automatic transmission as an option, to automatic as standard on many new car models?

Yet some changes leave us saddened. The death of a loved one is usually the most challenging time of growth. When my mother died, I was forty-six years old, and she was eighty-six. Her death made me stronger. I grew up some more. I no longer had Mama to listen to me and advise me. I had to make my own decisions work. But that was again an opportunity for self-empowerment.

I welcome new experiences, new words, new relationships, and new opportunities for self-empowerment because they prompt new revelations of inner spirituality and signs of growing up.

I've earned the right to be outspoken, bold, vain, and selfish.

Isn't it funny how some words change in meaning over time? Words such as "outspoken," "bold," "vain," and "selfish" used to describe negative traits, usually in women. Such words are still emotionally charged, but they have different meanings today. For example, during the days when women were to be seen and not heard, "outspoken" implied speaking out of turn. Today, the word is a compliment, suggesting that the speaker is confident and brave. But isn't it wonderful the power we have to redefine words to suit us!

"Bold" was a good word that used to apply to men's sense of adventure, their courage. Heaven help the woman who was called bold, however. Back then it was a big stamp of disapproval and hinted at a woman's embrace of the masculine rather than the feminine.

I've redefined the word "vain" for myself. "Vain" means "loving oneself." Loving oneself used to be considered selfish, but now we all know that before we can love others, we must first love ourselves.

Possibly the word that has received the most resistance to change from negative to positive is "selfish." This word was used to keep us in line. No one wanted to be considered selfish. So over the years, we often put other people's happiness before our own. If there was one slice of your favorite pie left, you gave it to your husband. Your head might have been splitting, but you climbed out of bed anyway to bake that batch of cookies for the school bake sale instead of driving to the nearest bakery. I'm happy to say that it's a new day.

I have earned the right to give only when it pleases me and to be selfish when it is in my best interest.

From this day forward I'll be honest about my feelings.

You tried not to rock the boat, so you said yes when you really wanted to say no. You didn't want to be thought of as a negative person. Lord forbid! You're a team player and very nice to be around. You never stop to question the other person's motives or his or her insensitivity to your needs.

I remember when I first retired, I received a flood of proposals to serve on a variety of boards. The pitch was, "Since you're retired, you have more time." I smiled politely but firmly stated, "No, thank you." After all, I retired to have more free time to explore new things. I'd had my fill of board and committee work. Folks are always kind of shocked to hear one "decline the opportunity to serve" without an apology. But I have found that an apology really invites the other person to evaluate whether my reasons for not serving are good enough. Instead I have been consistent with my noes, and it still feels good. Now my public service is as a volunteer consultant.

How about putting yourself first for a change? Is your desire to be liked so strong that you think you'll lose friends if you challenge them by saying no? The truth is that because you are so agreeable all the time, your friends might perceive you as weak, an easy mark. Learn to say no. Practice on your dog first, then graduate to human beings. Practice makes perfect.

I'll say no when I do not feel like fulfilling another's request because I have earned the right to be honest about my feelings.

34

My knowledge puts me ahead of being threatened by youth.

Sometimes I look at young people and shake my head. Thank you, Lord. I don't have to go through that again! Remember your first date? Your first final in college? Your first job interview? There are so many things that folks under forty fret about and question. I feel good saying, "Been there, done that, and don't ever have to do it again."

I still have some occasions to be anxious, scared, or questioning, but my fifty-plus years of experience after high school have taught me that I can face whatever life tosses my way with class and humor because I know that all I have to do is my best. The rest is up to God.

Someone said of youth, "If you do it right, once is enough." The anonymous speaker couldn't have been more right.

I enjoy the young, but I do not wish to return to my youth; I am pleased to be at this stage of my life.

I'll let go of things that I cannot change.

Do you know people who are worrywarts? They worry about real things—and not-so-real things. They worry about what-ifs. I sometimes think they invent situations to worry about. When they have a worry-free day, they worry that they are not worrying. It may sound crazy, but it's true.

I have a friend who must have a Ph.D. in worry. When he answers the phone, I can tell by the voice tension what level of worry he's into. He takes everything personally, even stuff that doesn't concern him directly. He has a worry for every subject, from the homeless to Fortune 500 millionaires.

For example, one day I called him and said, "Hi, what's up?" As soon as the words left my mouth, I knew I had asked the wrong question. "I don't know why every grammar school doesn't have enough computers," he said. He went on to expound on the fact that the new millennium demands that all children should be computer literate, and I agreed. When I suggested he adopt a school and work to raise funds to purchase computers, he had all kinds of excuses. I said, "If you don't plan to offer solutions to the situation, why worry about it? At least, don't talk to me about it." I've given up trying to show him the folly of his ways.

I will give a problem—or a worrywart—my best thinking, and then I will let it go.

36

The early part of life got me ready for the adventure of the last part.

Childhood, the teen years, and adulthood—all prepare you for the second half of life. Search out fond memories from each age. Then be reassured that the best is yet to come. No playing of games, no enforcing curfews, no participating in den mother activities, no holding your child's hand through the first broken heart, no hunting for the proper words to explain life and death.

The first thing I did when I retired from dance was to take oil painting classes. I wanted the paintings to be in my color scheme—blues, greens, and white. Today my original oils decorate my home. No one will mistake them for Rembrandts, but I'm pleased with the results. More recently I've been taking a class in stained-glass cutting, and I'm having a ball. I actually designed my first piece, an abstract guardian angel. I'm working now on a round window of a calla lily, my most difficult effort so far.

What is your next creative project? The second half of life is for exploring the interests that tweaked your curiosity in your busy, young years. Does your new venture seem unsuccessful? That's okay, because the fear of failure no longer controls you. You're exploring new things to satisfy your curiosity.

That's what the second half of life is all about—enjoying new pleasures, exploring new dimensions, learning new skills. Now you can travel more and not be limited to two-week vacations. You can take midweek minivacations. You can read a book just for fun. You can seek out all the pleasures life has to offer.

I will make each day an adventure by exploring interests that I have laid aside until now.

I'll celebrate honesty.

It seems George Washington's honesty is taught in every elementary school. He is supposed to have said, "I cannot tell a lie, I chopped down the cherry tree." It was a rare instance of truth-telling, especially in the face of possible punishment. Many historians regard this legend as having little historical basis, however.

True or not, it has become a touch-point for being honest with oneself and others. People's words should mean something. Yet lies do not seem to be shunned today. The little lies that make for social politeness have given way to untruthful denials and subterfuges. Younger—and older—persons say that it's no big deal.

How can you depend on people if you never know whether they're telling the truth? I call it throwaway talk. "Let's do lunch" is bandied about with no intention of establishing and keeping a luncheon date. "Let's get together real soon" is another throwaway. My pet peeve is hearing someone say, "I'll call you"—and then never receiving a call from that person.

When I say, "Let's do lunch", or, "Let's get together real soon," I stop to set up a date and time. I also make sure that the person has my number in case something comes up, and we have to cancel. We must go back to the old ways. Sticking to your word and telling the truth are good, strong values. Your word should be your bond.

I will celebrate honesty by saying what I mean and by honoring commitments.

38

I'll give a sincere compliment to someone today.

Giving sincere compliments can be a gratifying experience for you, the giver, as well as for the receivers. How? By recognizing the best in others and then letting them in on what you see. "You have such a pretty smile." "I appreciate your generous spirit." "Love that dress you're wearing!" "New hairdo? Wow! It's fabulous on you!"

The key to giving a compliment is sincerity. The better we know the other person, the easier it is to give her or him a true compliment. Sometimes we forget to compliment those closest to us—spouses, children, siblings, and parents—so go ahead, sprinkle the compliments around.

Then compliment strangers. They may be shocked at first, but if you give your compliment with sincerity, you will surely see their faces light up with surprise and joy. You put a smile on their faces, and you leave with a smile on yours.

Just as important as giving compliments is learning how to receive them well. Receiving compliments can be difficult for the insecure. Women who have just entered their second half of life can be full of insecurities. But many of us well into this time have trouble responding well to compliments, too. "What do you mean I look good in this dress? You see that I've gained five pounds." "Can't you tell that this is a bad hair day?" When others see the positive in you, resist the temptation to relapse into the old negative tapes. Learn to say thank you, and dare to believe that the person just might be telling the truth.

I will give at least one sincere compliment to someone, and if I'm lucky, I'll get to thank someone, too.

My good thoughts will convert to good feelings and health.

A statement seldom heard anymore is this: "You must have gotten up on the wrong side of the bed." Today people say, "What's the matter, you got your habits on?" or "Attitude, attitude, attitude." Translated, they all mean the same—bad mood.

Your moods are your responsibility. Saying, "He made me mad," or, "She got on my last nerve," means you're not in control of yourself. No one can make you anything. Only you can make you how you want to be—mad, sad, happy, or indifferent.

You have choices. Just because your family and friends have known you as short-tempered and unpleasant doesn't mean you have to stay that way. You have believed such bad press for too many years. Now that you're older, why not do a complete turnaround? Shock them all (and yourself) by becoming a positive, upbeat person. Those headaches that come when you get so angry will disappear. You'll feel better by keeping a slower heart rate and lowering your blood pressure.

What's the secret? You need to decide to make the change. Being congenial will feel strange at first. But stick to it, and enjoy the happiness and peace that come with good thoughts.

I will take responsibility for my feelings today by deciding to think and act in a positive, upbeat manner; doing this will convert into a healthier me.

40

I will celebrate birthdays with style.

Every year is precious and should be celebrated. That's what birthdays are all about. But certain ages are landmarks in life and deserve special attention. I can remember turning ten. Wow! I had two digits in my age, and I felt quite grown-up. I could stay up one hour later, too. The next landmark was age thirteen. The word "teenager" finally applied to me. Sweet sixteen is still a teenager, but a much more mature one. I grew up real fast on that birthday because the day I turned sixteen was December 7, 1941—the day Pearl Harbor was bombed.

Twenty-one, of course, was special because I could vote and was considered legally an adult. Birthdays continue to be fun now that I'm an adult. I've always believed that life begins at forty, so when I reached that landmark, I celebrated big time.

I continued making each birthday special. When I turned seventy, I really celebrated another landmark in my life. I jokingly told my friends that I would hire a Goodyear blimp to fly "Happy 70th to Ruth" high above the city and have fireworks shot off. I settled on a white-tie dinner party for two hundred close friends. I reserved the popular local supper club. It was a handsome night. I designed a mustard gold–colored velveteen form-fitting dress with long pointed sleeves, a turtleneck, and a train—yes, a train, and I knew how to kick it, too. When I took center stage, I invited everybody to my one hundredth birthday shindig.

As a woman in the second half of life, consider yourself blessed to be alive. Use each and every birthday to celebrate the high occasion of your birth and your precious life.

I will celebrate my birthday with style every year, and I will help other women celebrate their birthdays as well.

41

I'll bury old guilts and nurture the seeds of self-esteem.

Big problems are often described as weighty or burdensome. "That's heavy." "It's like a monkey on my back." "It's a load on my mind." "It's backbreaking." Problems real and unreal can make you feel loaded down. If each negative thought or action was a heavy brick packed in a suitcase, you might not be able to pick it up.

Where did those bricks come from? Think back. Most of the load is from the first thirty years of life. During that time in your life, you were trying to please everyone—parents, siblings, spouse, children, and coworkers.

Meanwhile the old tapes that say you're unworthy keep playing in your head. Perhaps in your childhood you were told, "Dummy, can't you do anything right?" "You're ugly [clumsy, etc.]. Why can't you be more like so-and-so?" Those tapes have added a number of bricks.

Sit down and make a list of all of your achievements and all of your physical assets. Don't hold back. List them all: a great smile, patience, honesty, high energy, loyalty, beautiful eyelashes—anything positive that you've ever heard or observed about yourself. Remember that a gift of years is honesty. So fill as many pages as necessary.

Now put down your pen and read your list. The more you read it over, the lighter your negative brick bag becomes. The lighter your load, the more upright you'll stand. The more upright your stance, the more you will be glad to be who you are. And that gladness is the feeling of self-worth.

I will make a list of my achievements and physical assets today, and I will read through it at least once a week—adding to my list as I embrace other qualities.

Now I have the courage to dig up secret ambitions and pursue them.

Is there something you've always wanted to do, I mean really wanted to do? What stopped you? Fear of embarrassment? Fear that you couldn't do it? If you let fear stop you, you'll never accomplish anything. Let's deal with your fear in baby steps.

First, investigate a beginner class that fits your schedule so that you can't cop out with a "conflict of schedule" excuse. Next, sign up. Then, go to the first class. That wasn't so hard, was it? Become a new you for the one or two hours that you're learning this new activity. Don't be concerned if you're the only student with gray hair or a wrinkle or two. You're there for your own pleasure.

Having been a professional dancer all my life, I had the secret ambition to be a lounge–type singer. You know the type: fabulous gowns, a smooth backup trio. I liked to imagine myself sitting on a stool that was nestled in the curve of a black–lacquered baby grand.

I was the only gray head in the local community college voice class, and I didn't miss a day. I loved it. When it was time for the end–of–the–semester production, I didn't flinch. I said, "Yes, I'll sing a solo." Well, it wasn't exactly a lounge, but my scene was a speakeasy of the 1930s. I stepped up to the mike in an elegant form–fitting dress with a slit all the way up the leg, and I sang. It wasn't exactly the love song I fantasized about, and I didn't have a backup trio. But it was actually me in front of a packed house singing.

I had a grand time. Were the shouts and loud applause genuine? I really didn't care. I had satisfied my secret ambition. Thinking about it still brings a smile to my face.

I will list my secret ambitions and make plans to pursue one of them in the next three months.

I'll listen to my inner voice and trusted friends a little more.

Couldn't you just give yourself a good swift kick? Earlier in life, spur-of-the-moment actions were the natural way to approach things. You skimmed quickly over the situation and snapped to a decision. Should a voice of concern try to intrude into your action, you pooh-poohed it and kept on with your original plan. "Wait, don't go in that direction," a little voice would cry out. "I know what I'm doing," you'd tell yourself, and then bang! The brick wall would rise up out of the blue, and you would crash smack-dab into it.

Years later, after several bumps on the head, you began to learn. The old impatience eased up. Now you ask questions of your trusted friends, such as, "How do you see things? Show me an alternative way." And you also pause to reflect whenever that little voice cries out. Instead of hitting brick walls, you see a pathway opening through the proverbial sea, and you calmly walk through it intact and unscathed.

What has happened to you? Why, you've learned to take in more information—and know that sometimes two heads are better than one.

I will trust my inner voice more as well as invite the opinions of my friends to guide me.

44

I no longer have the luxury of procrastination.

Did you have big dreams in the first half of your life? To start a career, launch a lifelong relationship, invest in a blue-chip portfolio, or make the world a better place? If you have accomplished even a portion of these dreams, then you are to be congratulated. But if your early dreams now prompt you to smile (or even laugh out loud), then it's time to rethink things. Women in the second half of life can no longer put things off. Even if our early dreams have faded, we need to act on more modest, realistic plans and get them done.

Frankly, I don't like dealing with procrastinators. They are a waste of my time and energy. They're always saying what they have yet to do. They can have all the spare time in the world, but they will still talk about how much they have to do. Why don't they just do it? But no, they wait until the last minute and then complain of the stress and pressure. Perhaps they love the urgency. Adrenaline is their motivation.

My motivation is the task itself, done in a cool, well-organized manner. Then I'm free, stress free. Tomorrow is not promised, and we'll all die at some point. When I hear about the death of an old friend, I wonder, "Did she get to do all she wanted to accomplish, or did she continue to think a thirty-year plan was realistic?" Sure, many people live longer today, and living to one hundred is more common, but isn't it kinder to yourself to have short-term goals and the reward of an immediate accomplishment? So, whatever it is you'd like to do, do it, and do it now!

I will realize my dreams by making plans and taking action; finishing each step gives me a boost because I no longer have time for procrastination.

45

I'll pamper myself whenever I feel like it, even if it means eating beans for a week.

Haven't you at times longed to escape to an elegant spa and be served while you just lie back and enjoy it all? No kids to carpool, no uptight boss, no spouse's ego to stroke, nothing to do but daydream and feel good? Even if you could have justified spending that kind of money on yourself, when would you have found the time? (I should think that the enjoyment of a proper mud bath can't be rushed.)

In the second half of life, you will have more time; if it doesn't show up on its own, then you know how to make time for yourself. Now pamper yourself. Perhaps you have never spent as much money as the deluxe treatment costs just to feel good. "Do I dare?" you might wonder. Wait a minute! You don't have to justify anything to anyone anymore.

So you call and get a reservation and take yourself to the best spa in town. You're smiling inside. You feel like a kid on an adventure. It is an adventure, and it's okay to feel like a kid. Several hours later you emerge feeling absolutely super from head to toe. Your skin glows, thanks to the mud bath (it wasn't gross, just warm and soothing). Your nails have a new hot color (might as well buy some cute sandals to show them off). Your face is baby smooth, and the arched eyebrows look great.

You decide then and there to repeat your adventure whenever the urge hits. And the beans? Well, they are a good source of protein!

Yes, I will treat myself to something special whenever I feel like it, even if it means I have to eat beans for a week.

In the mirror I see both the problem and the solution.

When you were closing in on forty-five, you didn't want to look in the mirror. You didn't want to see your reflection because it wasn't perfect. But this mirror was disturbing to you for another reason. Like an X ray, it saw your intentions, your plans, and your actions. It was able to see through the layers of denial, blame placing, and indecision, all things you hid from yourself.

The truth is that we can always find some justification for our actions. "I was too young." "Too old." "They were racist." "I didn't have a way to get there." All of these comments may be true, but what are you going to do about it? Do you give up and look for good enough reasons not to make additional progress in your life? Or do you take action to right the wrong?

Let your positive accomplishments offset your occasional failures. With your self-esteem firmly in place, the mirror becomes a tool for growth. The mirror becomes your friend. By now you've learned that the answers to all your problems are within. Deal with your problems courageously, one at a time.

I will look in the mirror each day to see my intentions and denials—and how I can grow by addressing my problems courageously.

47

I'll be as good to myself as I am to my best friend.

As life goes on, you cherish friendships more and more. But cherish yourself too. You know that your best friend values your honesty. Be honest with yourself, even when it hurts. You show your friend patience, even if it's hard to do sometimes. Self-patience is difficult, but necessary. Compassion is a given where your friend is concerned. Why is it so hard to be compassionate with yourself? You enjoy going out to lunch and dinner with your friends. It increases bonding. Choose your favorite restaurant, and be your own date often. Your friend values your dependability. You're always there. Depend on yourself. If it's okay for your friends, it's okay for you. You love your dear old friends.

When we are consciously destructive to our bodies, I wonder about our degree of self-love. I look at addicts and wonder what their self-dialogue was at the time of the very first snort or first needle prick or first drag on a cigarette. No one can claim ignorance these days of the bodily harm resulting from smoking or drug abuse. So, where is the love?

If you aim to truly love, then you must love your total self. It's never too late to start a love affair with yourself. Vow to clean up your act immediately. You are worth it.

Three self-love statements that I definitely live by are these: I owe it to myself to do such and such, even if it's frivolous; I work for my pleasures; and out of each paycheck I set aside a few dollars purely for personal enjoyment.

I love myself unconditionally, and I am my own best friend.

I won't take myself so seriously anymore.

When you were ten or eleven years old, people were always asking, "What are you going to be when you grow up?" You felt compelled to have some sort of answer ready. You heard your friends bragging about wanting to be doctors or lawyers, so you picked a career just to get the attention off yourself. "I'm going to be a firefighter, nurse, mama, doctor." Then came adulthood and making that career decision a reality. So you prepared yourself for your chosen grown-up career. No turning back—not with a family, a mortgage, and years of preparation behind you.

Take heart. No longer do you have to prove yourself to anyone anymore. Now, in your second half of life, you know who you are, and you are content with yourself. What a relief!

I will celebrate the increasing freedom of the second half of life by not taking myself so seriously.

49

*I've been a dormant bud too long—
it's my time to blossom.*

It took you more than fifty years to get the real you to stand up. You knew it was nestled deep inside, but you didn't dare come out of hiding. During those bud days, you were encased in the protective leaves of husband and children. The elements were unable to reach you; the rain, the frost, and the hot sun of the real world never reached your tender petals. You wondered what the raindrops of insecurity felt like, what the hot sun of a demanding career would do to your glow of color. For older women, husband and home were the throwbacks to the traditional values. Wives and mothers stayed and worked in the home.

Now you've decided it's your turn. Come what may, the kids are older or gone, and your husband will just have to take your coming of age in stride. Can this be you? You started out a couple of days a week at the community college, and you loved learning new things and meeting new friends. You do things that you enjoy, and you're even learning how to enjoy your own company. When your spouse comes home, a note tells him how to warm his dinner if you're late. You now wear your favorite colors, not only his. Your life is an adventure, not a routine. Your husband was so shocked that he couldn't figure out how to intelligently protest. At first he felt threatened, but he soon realized that your growth gave him a new freedom. He now enjoys living an interdependent life with you. It feels like a brand-new relationship, exciting and full of potential.

I will now try new things, experiment, and test myself because I know I cannot fail.

I'll challenge myself to venture into a new, unfamiliar activity.

Middle age can bring a certain smugness into your life. You're secure in the knowledge and demands of your career. You proudly look to the handiwork of your efforts in your beautiful, successful offspring. You have to admit that it was touch and go with them for a while, but your love and understanding patience won out. Things are okay, but you feel a need for something more. You need a challenge. Dare yourself to at least try something that will make you the student instead of the teacher. Not being in charge will feel so refreshing. No super–image to maintain. Be a sponge again and soak up new information.

I had never acted when I was invited to audition for the lead in a play. I was very reluctant. How was I going to memorize all those lines? Well, I got the lead, and I became a student of theater. I hadn't even done high school plays, so I didn't know any of the terminology that actors use. "You're going up on your lines," the director said. "What does that mean?" I asked. "You've forgotten some script." I mean, I knew how to project stage presence from my years of dancing, but I really felt insecure. But I'm a good student. I buckled down and applied myself to my new subject. I prevailed and actually got a good review. I'm still acting to this day and having fun from my second career in television and film. I call myself the "Cameo Queen." So swallow your misgivings and reexperience the excitement of learning.

Each day, I'll challenge myself to venture into new, unfamiliar activities.

51

I'll go with the flowing stream because now it's my turn to float.

What do the salmon and I have in common? We both swim upstream. In my dance career, it seemed I was always swimming upstream. Going against the tide as the first and only African American in the class or in the show was rough, but it was something I had to do. My career started during the days of vaudeville. I studied all kinds of popular dance, from acrobatics and ballet to toe tap and hula. From the age of five or six, I was preparing for the career I knew would be my life's work. From the age of three, when I started training, to my days at the University of California—Berkeley's physical education department and the Halprin/Lathrop Modern Dance School in San Francisco, I was always the center of curiosity. In the 1950s, my dance company was often the first concert African American dance company seen by our majority white audiences, who were more familiar with blacks in a night-club setting. Thank goodness, my family provided a nice, soft, cozy cushion to comfort and shelter me when I got home. Now that I'm retired from a very successful career, I can float with the tide. I have gladly passed the baton to some of my former students. It's now their time to forge upstream. My greatest joy is seeing them able to not only absorb my teachings but also exceed my expectations. I believe that students should eventually be even more accomplished than their teacher, especially if they have been given a firm foundation upon which to grow.

I have no more rivers to ford. It's my turn to float for a while.

I can face disappointment because I know it's a temporary condition.

As a young person, I took disappointment very badly, so badly that I was always the last one to know if a family outing was planned. If the outing was to be a fun day at the beach, I wouldn't know about it until the actual day because it might rain and I'd be crushed if we couldn't go. If I was told about an outing the night before we were to leave, I would set out what I planned to wear, gather up my toys, and put in my bid for my favorite snack. In short, I was totally ready, and if something uncontrollable and unforeseen prevented us from going, no one wanted to see my long face all tragic the next day.

Even as an adult, I find it hard to accept a change in plans, whether they are business or social. I have to continually work on myself to be more lenient with folks who break appointments. Meetings can be rescheduled, so what's the big deal? Now that I'm older, I realize that meetings need not be canceled, just postponed.

A broken heart, grief, death of a loved one, debt, unemployment, pain, and other soul-shaking episodes—these are all temporary conditions from which you will rebound and heal. They are not set in stone. Following my retirement from dance, and after my divorce, I found myself unemployed. It was a very uncomfortable feeling. While I was thankful for the unemployment insurance, I did not like dealing with the bureaucracy. What a drag. The clerks' air of superiority didn't help the situation either. Going on job interviews, selling myself, strict budgeting, and staying positive made me stronger, and I'm a better person for the experiences. It's an ongoing process.

I will try to be less controlling and more understanding when I am disappointed.

I decide which habits to retain or discard.

Some bad habits, such as nail biting, are a nuisance, but others, such as smoking cigarettes, can kill. The good habits that we've developed over the years are the ones we want to keep, for example, following a nutritious, low-fat diet and exercising regularly. Habits, whether good or bad, are developed in the same way—through repetition over time. They become a part of our personalities and our day-to-day routines. Still, we cannot allow our habits to get the best of us. We are in control of our lives, and we have the power to keep or let go of a habit.

For example, if you automatically light up a cigarette after eating lunch, then you know that you need to replace that bad habit with a good one, such as getting up from the table and taking a walk. Some say that a new habit can be created in twenty-one days; others say forty. The key is consistency and mental alertness to the possibility of sabotage.

Something I recently started doing was inspired by Stevie Wonder's "I Just Called to Say I Love You." Before I hang up from talking to my play daughters and when I see my grandnephew, Douglas, I tell them that I love them. It's a habit now, and I always think about what I'm saying.

It took a while to know that you were in control of your life, and it was a full-time job. You have choices to constantly make, but now you understand and love your-self enough to know that you deserve the very best. Create a new habit by starting each day with a positive plan. You're happier when your life is structured, so planning your time is a habit that can become automatic. Most important, strengthen the creation of a new habit through prayer and visualization—for example, imagine yourself exercising regularly or drinking eight glasses of water every day.

God strengthens my resolve. I am in God's care.

I am enthusiastic because enthusiasm has no age limit.

Act your age. Now just what does that mean? Who appoints the judges? What are the qualifications to become a judge? Are the judges self–appointed? The first judges are your parents. Do you remember hearing this? "Stop trying to act so grown up. I said no makeup." Or, "Trying to act like a woman doesn't make you one." Folks have a concept of what middle age or old age should be, and being outwardly demonstrative is not included. You're expected to be sedate, to be cool, and not show excitement in a physical manner. You can be feeling all bubbly inside, but you wouldn't dare jump up and down with enthusiasm. No, you wouldn't be acting your age.

Just saying that you feel excited about something can cause a brow to lift. You're supposed to have already experienced the gamut of emotions, so overreacting is not proper. Well, I am very improper. If I'm on the phone and persons don't know my age, they're always surprised to discover my true age because the energy in my voice makes me sound much younger.

I have two girlfriends, Dorothy and Brenda, who believe as I do that events should be celebrated. We use any excuse to get together to have a fabulous lunch. We celebrate birthdays, holidays, new business contracts, any success, fun trips, our friendship, you name it. Finishing this book called for a great celebration.

So show excitement. Be enthusiastic about big and lit- tle things. You are spirit, so shout, giggle, cry, smile, and clap your hands whenever the urge comes over you.

I will celebrate with friends, and I will shout, giggle, cry, smile, and clap my hands whenever I feel the urge.

55

Now that I am alone, my plan is to live.

First there's the shock. Then the anger, then the grief, and only then does the healing process begin. You ask yourself, "Where do I go from here? What do I do with all of my tomorrows?" Once the business of changing your name, signing legal documents, and so forth has been completed, then comes the hard part—facing the tomorrows. For a while, your life feels like a roller coaster, with deep, breathtaking falls and high peaks. Home seems so quiet, you leave on the television just for company. Cooking for one has no appeal, so fast foods, even TV dinners, become your diet. Friends are there for you, but you don't want to become a burden.

Sit yourself down and have a one-sided conversation. It might go something like this: "I must look for an activity to do regularly that brings meaning and purpose to my life. Volunteers are always needed. I have skills that I can volunteer. I mustn't wear out my role as grandmother. I'll force myself to cook my favorite dishes until I'm back into the cooking habit and my appetite returns. I must start on those books I bought and never had time to read. Now I'm my own high priority. I'm free to be whatever I choose to be on a day-by-day basis. My only discipline is to live, live, live!"

I will live each day alone with purpose and joie de vivre.

I'll take a big, bold step for a bold, new me.

At age forty-six you've decided to do a self-evaluation careerwise. Are you satisfied? You've been at the same job for twenty years. It's what you went to college to do, but for the past few years you've been feeling less motivated. You always wanted to be a nurse. You can remember as a little girl nursing your dolls. But years later, with thousands of dollars invested in your training, you're bored.

Your family has no inkling of your unrest. When your husband began to suspect that something was wrong, you pretended it was PMS. You're ashamed to say that you don't want to be a nurse anymore. Folks will surely think you're crazy. You are a supervisor, and you get good benefits. Even your salary is good. What you're forgetting is that God's plan for you is joy in your life. If eight hours of your day are joyless, you are not being true to yourself. Don't let the embarrassment of making a job change and starting all over again keep you in a stagnant position. Remember, you were capable enough to be successful in your chosen field, and that same intelligence can give you success doing something else.

Let's say you really want to teach. That's another worthy career with no shortage of jobs. I love teaching because I am really making a difference in people's lives. So, go for it and know that God is your partner.

I will no longer tolerate eight boring hours per day.

I'll get my Ph.D. in rest.

I am a professional when it comes to resting. I'm serious. I'm known as a "bed person." It's a very elite group, but I'm out to increase membership. I've recruited many folks. All you have to do is to follow my ten-step program. I have had many years of experience, hence my Ph.D.

My mother used to tell me that I would never die tired. You see, I started as a child prodigy in resting when I was about nine years old. I studied my dancing lessons kinesthetically, in bed. I did all my choreography and this book on a yellow tablet in bed.

Today my phone stays on my bed. I must say that I have a very good bed. It's a pillow-top king-sized bed that raises head and foot and shimmies and shakes. You don't need all of that, but you must be comfy.

Rules and regulations:

1. Get over feeling guilty about being in bed during the day.

2. You must be organized to accrue free time. You get no "bed points" if you're in bed thinking about what you should be doing. Only a clear conscience is allowed in bed.

3. Even if you have only one hour, grab one hour of bed rest.

4. Get out of binding clothes. No restriction of blood vessels is allowed. No bras, belts, panty hose, or jewelry.

5. Resting in a chair doesn't count. Only resting in bed is valid.

6. Note: Rest is not sleep, but body rest.

7. Don't think of rest as "wasted time." It's healing time.

8. You can turn on the radio, music, or TV if the silence scares you.

9. If you can, work in bed. For example, you can balance your checkbook, plan events, make business calls, and so forth.

10. The goal is for your body to slow down for a while. Let yourself breathe, and let your blood circulate without gravity pulling on your body.

Now take the pledge: "I, [your name], promise as a Bed Buddy to follow rules 1 through 10." Welcome to my club. You are now a Beckford Bed Buddy.

I will strive to be a faithful Beckford Bed Buddy.

58

"Stress" is definitely a baby-boomer word. I don't recall hearing folks during the 1930s depression saying they were stressed. I was a WWII teen in Oakland. Military bases were everywhere. I didn't hear anyone say, "I'm stressed out." Those were really stressful times, but folks dealt with it. The other day, I heard a little girl, about five years old, say to her mother, "I'm stressed out."

When you say you're stressed, it's an abdication in most instances because you stress yourself. You allow it to happen. You let your environment dictate to you. You just go along, getting increasingly angry and worried.

Stop right now, and take control of everything you can control, especially your thoughts and emotions. Reflect on the occasions of greatest stress. Usually work makes this list. If every Monday is painful and all weekend you're worried about the coming week, then you need to go into your self-closet and stay there until you can come out with some truths. (Beckford Bed Buddies can use their beds.)

Ask yourself if your job is really painful or if you are just used to griping along with your coworkers. If it is really bad, then take compensation time, sick leave, or a vacation day to job hunt. Find something you have a passion for, and apply. If you need training, then go to night school and get it. Don't quit your present job until the ink is dry on an offer letter for the job of your choice.

If your stress is in your home, the kids, and/or your mate, learn to say no sometimes. Stop being a super-mom, super-spouse, super-homemaker. Allocate duties. It'll build strong character. Or let the dust stay there for a while. It's okay. If the kids are in school, take yourself to a grown-up movie. A steady diet of animated cartoons can make for animated brains.

Sound time management will knock out mounds of stress. Draw a big clock face, and make a pie chart of your day and night. Save some bits of downtime for yourself, even if it's only ten minutes in the bathroom. Take your breaks at work by walking around the block alone. Plan your day the night before, including your wardrobe, so you don't hit the ground running. Arrive at work fifteen minutes early to give yourself transition time to pass from personal to professional. You're rattled all day if you don't have a little chill-out time.

From this day forward, stop saying, "I'm stressed out." Thoughts are things. Don't own stress. It is not a part of the real you. You are too together to let stress manipulate you. Rough times may come, but you can handle them. You're still here, so you've done something right. Just know that life can be even better with your new attitude.

I will stop using the word "stress."

59

Tick tock, you can stop the clock.

Panic is beginning to set in. For whatever reason, you put off having children. Perhaps you wanted to get your career under way. Maybe you're divorced now. Or perhaps you're seeing more friends in live-in relationships who choose not to have children.

Women are having babies in their forties, but is that how you want to enter into the second half of life? Are you ready for the 2:00 a.m., 4:00 a.m., and 6:00 a.m. feedings followed by a challenging day at work? Do you have what it takes to mother an infant? A lot of single parents are not parents by choice, but you do have a choice when you consider all of your options.

I was in a TV commercial for the Black Adoption Agency, and the storyboard began with an eight-year-old boy sadly peering through a window at a traditional family grouping of a mother, father, son, daughter, and grandmother. The point of the commercial was to make people aware of the great need to adopt older children. It's an overlooked option. It's a chance to be a loving parent with some of the early work of toilet training, bottle feeding, and teething eliminated. Bonding, in time, becomes just as strong. You even have a choice of adopting sisters and brothers if you want more than one child. You are needed. Think about it.

Tick tock, I can stop the clock.

Part Three

Romance

groovin'

60 My romantic spirit never ages.

61 I'm not limited to old beliefs.

62 I'll place less importance on the package and more on the gift.

63 I'll take a risk because I've got nothing to lose.

64 A tidal wave of love can start with a ripple.

65 I'll go out among people more often, even when I don't feel like it.

66 I'll consider a younger lover who is good, fun-loving, and honest.

67 I see myself as sexy—I have a sexy attitude.

68 I will be confident and phone for a lunch date.

69 Men may come and go, but girlfriends are forever.

70 I'll give looks that say, "I want to know you better."

71 I'll not fall in love anymore, but enter relationships on steady feet.

72 Even though I'm over forty-five, I will have safe sex.

73 I'll not date a person who wants a caretaker.

74 I'm sagging, but my date's eyesight isn't as sharp anymore either.

75 In soft light, my lines fade away.

76 I can still feel sixteen with the right person.

77 Longevity alone in a committed relationship is not a cause for celebration.

78 A relationship can succeed when each is excited by the other's interests.

79 I'll have the courage to end any relationship that gives me no joy.

80 I'll visit the community center, especially the social dance classes.

81 When my heart goes pitter-patter, I'm not having a coronary.

82 My next love will be a splendid thing.

83 Has the party animal lost her bite?

84 My last chapter remains to be written—a great romance novel?

There may be snow on the roof, but there's a fire blazing in the oven.

After age forty–five, incidences of separation, divorce, and widowhood increase. Moving from being part of a couple to being alone can make for a tough time of adjustment. It can feel like starting all over again. Before you might have said "we" and "us"; now you might need to say "me" and "I." Gone might be the reminder to change the oil, the surprise of a favorite meal cooked as you like it, being held as you fall asleep. But gone also is someone whose well–being must be your first concern.

A disappointment in a relationship can make us cautious about seeking out another companion. The idea of putting our trust, time, and energy into a new relationship can seem daunting. After the initial grief and anger have subsided, our newfound freedom can also be quite seductive. Many women choose not to marry again, feeling comfortable having casual relationships. But more than a few women spend the second half of life attempting to recover or regain what they seem to have lost.

The level of romantic feelings may surprise many women, especially seniors. But we can be romantic after age forty–five. Contrary to what popular culture would have us believe, young people have not cornered the market on love and romance. Do you remember thinking that seniors have long forgotten love and intimacy? Surprise! Now you will discover that we can make love and be in love—these get better with age. When it comes to sexual play and intercourse, experience is valuable. A healthy older person can be just as exciting as a younger person. We are less inhibited, more willing to be free with our sensuality. And soon (or already), we can't get pregnant.

What could be better? No living from menstrual cycle to cycle. No kids to hide from or watch out for. We're more compassionate and sharing, more honest with what we want and more willing to ask for it. Love grows from a deep place. We already have most of the things we need, so we're not chasing after the next pay raise or the last sale catalog. In the second half of life, we can feel good just being together, sharing the day's events, cuddling, snuggling—holding each other. By now, you know that if the relationship doesn't work out, you'll be fine, and life will go on. And you know that you do not need to invest twenty or thirty years in it.

Experiment. Allow yourself to really feel. Take the first step. Be courageous. It's never too late to have your first orgasm (or second or third, all on the same night). But safe sex is a must.

My romantic spirit never ages.

Where did the years go? You used to hear the older people say that and wondered why they always made that comment. Now you know. Everything still seems so fresh in your memory. You can almost smell the bridal flowers, the baby's dusting powder, the smoke from your first burned meal you tried to surprise your husband with.

The wonderful thing is that you still get a thrill when you think of your spouse. You now prepare unburned, surprise meals. You still get to select the movie you and he see together. He sends you flowers, and the card says, "I'm yours." It's pure romance. You know what the secret is: he listens to you, just as he did when you were dating. He is not too busy to give you a hug or to hold you until you fall asleep. He grabs your hand when you walk down the street. Yes, he even gives you an occasional massage. What more could you want? Not one single thing.

I will remember to tell my mate that I love him, and I will act accordingly.

61

I'm not limited to old beliefs.

You're white, so you won't date a black person. Or you're red, so you won't date a yellow person. You're brown, so you won't date a white person. Or you're black, so you date only black persons. You're not a racist, of course; it's just that race mixing is simply not done! You are comfortable with your decision.

But as you age, you realize how much you've been limiting yourself. You've associated with other races at work and play, why not in romance also? Yes, racism is stupid, and you're not ashamed to admit it. The fear is gone. Now you know that the old myths are untrue. True love is so rare and fragile, you know that to find it at all in a lifetime is a blessing. You know that all races of human beings are just plain human beings, good and bad alike. So, you'll now date whomever you can respect, trust, enjoy, and share a good laugh with.

I am open to relationships with persons of other races and ethnic traditions.

I'll place less importance on the package and more on the gift.

The greatest mystery used to be why the shortest man was with the tallest woman, or the skinniest woman with the fattest man. Two unattractive people were never together—one was always exceptionally gorgeous. Did you ever wonder what they saw in each other? Wasn't one embarrassed by the other? What was the attraction?

Such thoughts were the expression of your immaturity. It took you years (perhaps the first half of life?) to understand what was important. The odd couples already knew what it took you so long to realize—that we're all God's most whole and perfect children, and we're all deserving of love.

Maybe this time around, you'll be willing to get to know a person before automatically declining an invitation to go out. Regardless of the package, the important part of romance is chemistry that each can spark in the other. Sometimes it may be slow showing itself. Be patient. Leave behind in the first half of life the attitudes about who is or isn't your type. Thank goodness, you've grown up, or you could again have shortchanged yourself and missed a lot of genuinely fine relationships. You are now with age a more sensitive, intelligent person.

I will place less importance on the package and more on the gift inside.

63

I'll take a risk because I've got nothing to lose.

I couldn't believe I was going out on a blind date. I never went on blind dates before. Why now? First of all, men are more scarce. Second, my friends were certain that we'd really click. "Try it, you might like it," they said. But what if I didn't? Usually I stay clear of fix-ups, but they seemed so confident, I finally said okay.

My date rang the bell on time. (Yes, I could hear echoes of my mother when I was much younger and dating the first time around: "Keep him waiting a few minutes. Don't be so anxious!" His promptness did please me, since I'm always on time, too.) He was a nice-looking, well-dressed man with a great smile, and he was much taller than I. Well, as the old saying goes, "It wasn't a love connection, but it was a friend-boy connection." We had a lunch date. (This is my rule: meet your blind or personal-ad date at a public place for coffee or a drink. If a friend has set up the connection, lunch is okay, then have him pick you up.)

When we got to the restaurant, we ordered. Even though he was a professional, I took my cue from the cost of his order. (Is that too old-fashioned? No, maybe it's just civil.) He was generous and fun to talk to. He had two children with his ex-wife. I could see that his children were important, and I also saw that he was still angry over the divorce. I felt he needed time to heal. He didn't need me to complicate his life even more. We enjoyed good conversation and had a lot in common, but I just didn't feel any chemistry. He'll be a good friend, and who knows? Time may bring the chemistry, too.

I'll take a risk today because I have nothing to lose.

A tidal wave of love can start with a ripple.

I always shop at the same supermarket, usually the same day of the week, and the most convenient time is 7:00 a.m. The aisles aren't crowded, and checkout lines are short. Preparations for shopping are few. Grab my list, throw on sweats, and off I go. The last thing on my mind is a romantic encounter. I'm squeezing the lettuce when my eye happens to catch a rather handsome man doing the same thing. I select my lettuce and move on. After a few minutes, I notice he's where I am again. This time he smiles and nods. I smile and nod, and move on. Hmm, he's kind of cute, I think. The next week he's there again at the meat counter. He's buying chicken and I am, too. "I see you're a drumstick lover," he says. "Yep, I prefer buying just the parts I like." "Me too," he says.

This time I'm feeling an ever-so-slight quickening of the heart. A little temperature increase and a ripple in the chest. It's so faint, I'm not really sure it happened. What could be next? I pooh-pooh the feelings and halfheartedly try to convince myself that at my age I'm imagining the whole thing. Next week, though, I'll shop the wine and cheese section. Who knows? A sip of wine, some soft music...

As I go through my daily routine, I will be sensitive to single ripples—and enjoy them.

65

I'll go out among people more often, even when I don't feel like it.

Retired at last. No more demands on your time. You are free to go, stay, sleep late, or stay up all night. When you were employed, you interacted with the public in a smiling, positive manner eight hours a day for years. When you were at home, you didn't want to answer the phone. You felt talked out. When the children were living at home, they monopolized the phone, which was fine with you. Your husband was a rather quiet type, so you could just be quiet and think.

When your husband died, you found yourself alone and with nothing to do. It took some getting used to, but now you're beginning to enjoy your solitude so much that your friends and family are wondering what's the matter with you. They call to make sure you're okay. They are upset that you've been cutting them out of your life. They love you.

And although solitude can be bliss sometimes, you must admit that from time to time you get lonely for companionship. When you first became a widow, you never thought you'd ever say that.

It's a new day! Time to become a new you. Remember, thoughts are things. If you think you are old and over the hill, then you are. But if you think and know in your heart that you are alive, still sexy, and young at heart, then you are!

Focus on romance. If there is no companion around, then go to romantic movies. Give your wardrobe a new lift. Get back in touch with your sensuality. Look at men, all men, again and with an open mind. Read romance novels, take bubble baths, and even rent videos. So put a smile on your face and a strut to your walk. You go, girl!

I will go out among people more often, even when I don't feel like it.

66

I'll consider a younger lover who is good, fun-loving, and honest.

I don't date older men or even men my own age because they tend to live in the past; they reminisce constantly. They're usually more fragile, and they fall asleep early. No, I don't want any man as old as I am.

My first play—which was so successful that it became the first of a trilogy—was about the relationship between an upper-middle-class widow and an equally successful younger, handsome man. Let's say that I got the idea from real life. But the surprise was the number of women who came backstage to confess to me their younger-man relationships. (Some even had their men with them.)

"Gigolo," "protégé," "gold digger," and "nephew"—these are all terms used to describe the younger man. (Interesting how such terms are never used to describe the older man who is involved with a younger woman.) But this is a new day. Today's younger man can be sophisticated and financially secure. As older women strive to maintain youthful attitudes and appearances, younger men are attracted to their self-confidence, security, and strong sense of self. Younger men like the fact that with older women, there tends to be less game playing. For older women who have a high energy level and are willing to experience new things, the younger man is a perfect complement. Sexually, the older woman and the younger man are well-matched as long as he doesn't want children.

The late, great comedienne Moms Mabley said it best: "The only thing an old man can do for me is to bring me a message from a young man."

I will not ignore my option to date younger men.

I see myself as sexy—I have a sexy attitude.

The stereotype of being sexless just because you're older is fading away. The media now presents older couples holding hands, riding bikes, dancing. Seniors are no longer restricted to commercials that sell life insurance, denture cleansers, hair dyes, and wigs. We live longer, healthier lives.

Stop thinking of yourself the way you thought of your parents. I remember going into a lingerie shop that specialized in sexy underwear. The twenty-something, slim, cute clerk's best smile seemed more like a smirk when she asked, "Something for your daughter?" I replied with a question, "Do you carry larger sizes, too?" "Oh, yes, of course we do," the clerk said warmly. "Is she full-figured?" "Yes, I am. It's for me."

Well, I thought she was going to faint. Her face turned red, and her mouth dropped open. I asked her to take a breath. She mumbled out, "For…you…?" I tried to hold in my laugh, but I couldn't. I said, "One day, my dear, if you're lucky, you'll get to be my age. Then you'll know that being sexy has no age limit." I made my purchase and left. (Poor child. She's probably still in shock.)

Get involved in activities in which the opposite sex participates, but only if they interest you. You don't want to flirt with, say, a bowling fanatic if you hate bowling. Treat yourself to a bubble bath and step into new, sexy nightwear. When you dress in a sexy outfit, with all the accessories, you feel sexy. You exude sex and it's like a signal. Men get the message. You can be in jeans and a sweater, but because you feel sexy, your signal is strong. You're too intelligent and experienced for one-night trysts, but you want to be prepared when the special person finds you.

I will see myself as sexy, wear sexy undergarments, and cultivate a sexy attitude.

68

I will be confident and phone for a lunch date.

Our mothers taught us how to deal with males. But their lessons boil down to one thing: let the man be the initiator. Let him provide the transportation on a date. Wait for him to call you. How many times did you sit by the phone, praying the woman's phone prayer, "Oh, please, let him call me"? Our most forward behaviors were batting our eyelashes, giggling, and agreeing with every-thing he said.

There are some benefits to being older and freer. We can now initiate a date. We can call a man and schedule a time together—without sacrificing our feminine mystique. We may get turned down, but more often than not, men will be flattered and requite our interest with pleasure. It makes them feel good, handsome, and virile.

Because of my "hometown celebrity" status, some men are too intimidated to approach me. I saw an interesting man at a dinner party, spoke to him after I caught his eye, and got his card. Later that week, I called him, and we talked for an hour. I decided we had enough in common to pursue a relationship. When I asked him out to lunch, I paid the tab. He was flattered. He said he never thought I would consider a date with him, so he never asked. He'd known of me (although I didn't know him). He is still a close friend today, a good friend–boy.

I will be confident enough to phone for a lunch date because I am old enough to make up my own mind about what I want.

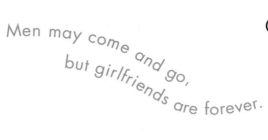

Men may come and go,
but girlfriends are forever.

Thank goodness for my girlfriends! Where would I be without their love, sympathy, and support during my most trying times?

Over the years we've shared the same anxieties, triumphs, and secrets. We've gone through broken hearts, marriages, divorces, childbirth, and illnesses together. We speak the same language. We think many of the same thoughts. Even in the midst of a passionate love affair, we cannot neglect one another.

I can remember after my second (and last) divorce, one of my best girlfriends picked me up and took me to a spa in northern California. We had a mud bath, a fabulous hour-long massage, and a great lunch. It was indeed a healing day, and only a real sister-friend would have been sensitive enough to understand my need.

When men get together, it's a guy thing, which may be fine for them, but hardly meets a woman's needs. Men seldom understand women's need to gather among themselves to vent, gossip, and share intimacies. Both men and women are from Earth, but most of the time women understand each other's vulnerabilities because we are sisters and we share them with one another.

I will continue to nurture my female friendships because we speak the same language.

I'll give looks that say, "I want to know you better."

You know you have something in common because you see him in church every Sunday. He's always busy, dealing with the collection plates, signing up new members, or leading prayer. He seems to be liked by everyone. It's been so long since you had a man in your life, you don't know where to start or what to do. He always comes alone—you've checked that out already. He's well-dressed. You even checked his socks length when he had his legs crossed. He passed that test too. (Don't you just hate the look of sock, then leg, then pants?)

You find yourself really looking forward to Sunday mornings. You take even more time with your wardrobe. You sit so that you can observe him as he goes about his duties. You begin to fantasize about your first date with him. Just the word "date" makes you giggle to yourself. (Is it still called a date when you're older?) You know he has seen you, but he hasn't made a move.

Out of the corner of your eye you catch him watching you too. Now what? You're a woman of the present, and it's now acceptable to make the first move, so drum up your courage and go for it!

I'll pull my shoulders back, raise my frown to a smile, and give out looks that say, "I want to get to know you better."

I'll not fall in love anymore, but enter relationships on steady feet.

Picture yourself falling down a deep well. You're out of control. You're grasping for a branch, but it's just out of reach. You're wondering how you even stumbled onto this well. You're a city woman. This is strange territory. You hit the bottom.

Patiently, bit by bit, you cut steps and handholds up the sides and climb out. You're bruised, but still in one piece. You ask yourself, "What am I doing way up here on this cliff?" You don't remember driving to the mountains, especially this high up. You glance over the edge. Oops! You're falling down a sheer cliff into the valley below. You hit bottom again, but this time the drop knocked the wind out of you, so you had to lie there a while to catch your breath.

It was a longer trail back to the top because you had to make your way spiraling round and round the mountain over rough terrain. By the time you're on safe ground, you have deep cuts, a sprained ankle, a dislocated shoulder—in short, you've been through a lot.

Falling in love can be like falling down a well or a steep cliff. No more, thank you. You have a map and a compass. Surprise turns are now fun, not deadly, thanks to life experience. Plan your trip in love cautiously. Your steps are only on firm, well-trodden earth.

I know my love trip will be a smooth journey because I will read the road signs carefully.

72

Even though I'm over forty-five, I will have safe sex.

Some younger folks are sexually active, but many teenagers now remain celibate until marriage. The seemingly old-fashioned moral code is important to them and still important to you.

One-night stands are not your style, and perhaps never have been. Even so, it can be tricky dealing with middle-aged and older men's attitudes. They consider safe sex something for young persons, not for them. They believe that because they aren't as active, they're safe. They also believe that all their partners are monogamous to them. The male ego seems to remain self-centered because men also believe that an older woman couldn't attract more than one man at a time.

Don't fall off your chair laughing. Safe sex is a rule that applies to men and women of all ages. If you're going to indulge in any kind of sex, you must use protection, no matter what your age.

Even though my fertility has diminished (or ceased), whenever I do have sex, it must be safe, protected sex.

I'll not date a person who wants a caretaker.

Older men who are dating are oftentimes widowed, divorced, or married. Let me lecture for a moment. Don't get involved with a married man. Are you so desperate to have a man that you are willing to be alone on holidays and weekends, waiting for him to squeeze you in? "But he says that he is about to get a divorce," you protest. Then let him make a clean break with his spouse before you get involved.

Older men, especially those who are widowed or divorced, are used to being catered to. They long for the stability of wholesome cooked meals, laundry done, house cleaned, and so forth. Men today, whether young or old, are more helpful around the house—as they should be— but they won't say no to a woman who volunteers to cook and clean.

Women in the second half of life can get snared into doing the first half of life a second time. Two examples come to mind. First, when we are in love, we tend to blossom with the urge to nurture. We can't wait to fix that candlelight dinner and put those rose petals in the bed. We are romantics. But early in your dating, be aware of the man who readily and too often suggests that the two of you have a quiet dinner at your place. He may even kick in for the groceries and the wine. Keep those elegant and not-so-elegant restaurant reservation numbers handy. Let home cooking be a special treat that you orchestrate on your own terms.

Second, a man can be a baby when he becomes sick. If he gets a cold, for example, then he can act as though he has pneumonia. Do you want to nurse his ills? Beware of the caretaker trap. Be concerned and helpful, give him a list of home care services, but don't let him move in with you—until you are ready.

I will not date someone who wants a caretaker—been there and done that already.

I'm sagging, but my date's eyesight isn't as sharp anymore either.

Spare tires, love handles, flabby muscles—as we age, our bodies begin to show signs of gravity's pull. Childbearing, illness, grief—life's major milestones often wreak havoc on our bodies. Those are the moments when we neglect to care for our bodies. We have to work harder to reclaim our bodies' natural healthy condition. We have to accept the fact that we won't look the way we did when we were twenty.

What you don't have to accept is that because you're a few pounds heavier, no man will ever be attracted to you. Are you finding that it's harder to lose weight now that you've gotten older?

Even when I do all the right things, I'm lucky to drop one pound a week. It's so easy to just give up, but my ego kicks in and I'm once again counting the grams of fat and doing my walking. I love to design my own clothes, and I'm determined to keep my hourglass figure, even if the dimensions are a little extended.

Men love women. It makes no difference whether you're overweight or thin, tall or short, gray-haired or whatever. Romance happens in the mind first. When you think you're attractive, you are.

I saw a talk show that had a sexy lingerie fashion show for full-figured women. But the models were pencil thin. The men who were there with their heavier mates selected the outfits for them to model. The surprise was that when

their mates came out in their sexy baby dolls and loung-
ing wear, the men whooped and cheered. They all wanted
their rounded women over the fashion models. So we can
still be very attractive to men, even with extra poundage.

I won't worry that I could use a nip here or a tuck there
because his eyesight isn't all that sharp anymore either.

In soft light, my lines fade away.

You're at an intimate restaurant with your date. Candlelight and soft music create a wonderful romantic atmosphere. Or you're at home. The two of you are watching TV together, and only the soft, flickering light from the set fills the room.

Lighting can create or burst the romantic mood. Lighting designers for live theater productions are paid well to evoke a mood. But you don't have to be a technician to switch from a 100-watt bulb to a softer, gentler light. A dimmer is also a good way to shift from bright to romantic with a simple touch of the finger.

One evening when I wanted to make a "wow!" impression, I used only candle lighting in the whole house, even in the kitchen. The effect was beautiful, and the slightly scented candles intensified the effect. The candles were all sizes, colors, and shapes. That creativity helped to shape an important relationship.

I will use soft lights to mute my wrinkles.

76

I still have the anticipation and excitement that automatically come with a new romance in my life. I still find myself thinking of him at odd times—while I'm doing the dishes, taking a walk, showering—but it's not with the same insecure urgency.

Any self-doubt is countered by reviewing my past experiences; I bring a full plate of good stuff to any relationship. I'm at peace with myself and don't have to prove myself to anyone else. I no longer put a man on the hot seat, grilling him about the lack of phone calls at this or that time.

Because I know my value and what I bring to a relationship, I am no doormat. I no longer tolerate bad or indifferent behavior. For example, I have noticed that his memory can be excellent when it comes to keeping business appointments or reserving seats at a basketball game, but it can become feeble when it comes to canceling a date. His forgetfulness signifies to me that he is not only inconsiderate of my feelings but also might not have a strong interest in the relationship.

When I was sixteen, I might have tolerated this behavior. Now that I am much older, I shall end any relationship that does not reflect my love as worthy of a high priority. I know I deserve the best, and you do, too. Don't settle for a disrespectful relationship just so you won't have to spend time alone. Expect that the love, honesty, maturity, passion, and respect that you bring to the relationship will be reciprocated.

I will insist upon respectful treatment even when someone makes me feel young again.

Longevity alone in a committed relationship is not a cause for celebration.

Think of all the twenty-four-hour segments that go into a twenty-year marriage. It boggles the mind. Anniversaries celebrate the annual pieces, but the day-to-day segments count most.

If you're married, then think back to the time when you swore to yourself that your marriage would never become routine. You were going to always have on your makeup, prepare romantic dinners, be a sex kitten every night, and be the supportive spouse to whatever ventures your husband undertook.

Surprise! Marriage isn't like that. Sometimes there's romance, but not on a twenty-four-hour basis. Part of the enjoyment of marriage is being able to relax and be yourself without the drama of dating. You feel free to go without makeup at home and have no fear of a breakup. You can have a disagreement and still be partners. You don't serve romantic dinners every night. You just want the kids to have a good, nourishing meal. You realize that the day-to-day events bring the partnership to the twentieth or fiftieth anniversary. You are each other's support system. You wouldn't trade one twenty-four-hour period for anything else.

I will make every twenty-four hours of my marriage a comfortable, loving down payment to many years together.

78

A relationship can succeed when each is excited by the other's interests.

Togetherness has probably destroyed more marriages than one would care to count. Think about all those two-somes squished together on Noah's ark. Or think about all the twin-wedding-ring ceremonies in which she takes his last name to signify the partnership. And step by step, two persons get squeezed into one togetherness: She tries to like what he likes, eat what he eats. Sleeping patterns, television programs, radio stations—the couple attempts to synchronize all interests and schedules.

But now you have reached the second half of life. You should feel secure enough to maintain and develop yourself; encourage your mate to do the same. Cloning each other can become boring. Having a variety of activities makes for fuller persons and interesting conversation. Today, persons come together as a couple because they have common goals. Each has his or her own agenda. Each shares the other's space because they want to, not because they have to.

As I develop my skills and interests, I will share my enthusiasm with others, but I will not feel threatened when an interest is not shared.

I'll have the courage to end any relationship that gives me no joy.

"I can't believe they're getting a divorce. They've been married more than twenty years." How many times have you heard (or said) this? Today, more and more married women are stepping back and taking a good, clear look at the past, the present, and especially the future.

Are you in a marriage that suffers from lack of love, caring, and mutual respect? Let's say that you've reexamined his one-time infidelity. He swore it was a brief encounter and promised to be faithful forever, and you believed him. Both of you had counseling, but you never quite got over the hurt or fully trusted him again.

Or maybe your marriage has no outstanding problems. It's just predictable and boring. The moments before his arrival home from work are your happy times. Now you're beginning to visualize being single all the time. You're making plans. You're looking for a higher-paying job because financial insecurity has been your main fear. When you get that job—when finances are no longer a problem—will you admit out loud what you've been denying? That you're not in love anymore?

When you deal with your fears, the truth of your marriage will make itself known to you. Maybe it can be saved, but maybe it can't. You'll never know unless you acknowledge and work on your fears and guilt. "Did I do or not do what was expected of me?" "How will I tell my adult offspring?" "How will I support myself?" "Will my close friends choose sides?" Do you want the rest of your life to be a lie? Do you deserve more? Yes, you do. Courage—take it. You'll be glad you did.

I'll have the courage to work on any negative relationship or end it, should long-term improvement not be forthcoming.

I'll visit the community center, especially the social dance classes.

I originally wrote "senior center," but my editor changed it to "community center." Hmm. And I thought that "senior center" sounded better than "old folks' center."

Maybe you don't like the way that sounds, either. Especially for women just entering the second half of life, perhaps the local gym or YWCA sounds more appealing. Or maybe you've been leaning into the second half of life for a while, but have resisted going to the "community center." Either way, you get lonely on the days when your girlfriends disappear there. Perhaps they have spoken of the new aerobic exercise or social dance classes. But you don't need any more toning or social toe-tapping. You're already good.

Out of curiosity, however, you decide to take the plunge and go. Wow! They didn't say the trainer was so caring or the dance teacher was such a good-looking widower. All of a sudden you decide you need to establish a complete training program at the gym or learn all of the dance fundamentals, especially the tango.

That's what happened to a close friend. She found that the dance instructor was more than a willing teacher. There was something about the way he held her while explaining how the tango is the dance of love that made her skin quiver with goose pimples. During intermission her friends pounced on her with friendly envy. "We've been here every week; you come once and get all the attention." They all laughed, and my friend had a renewed feeling of how nice it is to flirt and to be flirted with in return.

I'll visit the community center (gym, senior center) in order to improve my circulation.

When my heart goes pitter-patter,
I'm not having a coronary.

As we get older, any instant change in temperature or heartbeat is attributed to menopause. I think menopause is the catchall for any disorder. It is important to pay attention to our bodies and when we detect an irregularity to pursue it with a physician.

When my heart seemed to beat irregularly, I couldn't think of what could have caused it to skip beats. I knew it wasn't permanent because it settled down after a while. Looking back, I know that this may have been a foolish decision, but I decided to test it to see what caused the rapid, irregular beat. I did a vigorous stair-step routine. True, my heart rate increased, but it was a regular, faster beat. The beat gradually slowed as I cooled down. I tried power walking and swimming. Same results.

What caused my heart to skip beats? I gave up. I went on to prepare for my date with my newfound love. Everything was fine. I was in a new outfit, and I was feeling happy about the evening. The doorbell rang. I went to the door and opened it. Thumpity thump, skippity skip, thump, skippity skip, thump. Mystery solved.

Sometimes when my heart goes pitter-patter, I'm not having a heart attack; I'm just in love.

82

My next love will be a splendid thing.

Love is wonderful. True love should make you feel good. Love of parent for child is a must in order for the child to grow into a healthy, secure individual. Love between friends has unmatched loyalty and dependability. The love of mates is a precious love that only time can create. Good old-fashioned marriage is a bond that is unmatched. Caring for each other through thick and thin, in sickness and in health, as the vow states, really happens. Each test survived is another cemented brick in the couple's foundation. The closeness to the point of almost anticipating each other's thoughts becomes commonplace. Some longtime couples even take on each other's mannerisms and grow to look alike. They become one.

But for those of us who are taking the step into love again, love is both wonderful and not so wonderful.

It's like being a teenager minus the insecurity about his love. You know he loves you. You have trouble concentrating on things other than your new love. "What's he doing now?" "Is he thinking of me, too?" "He was so sweet when he told me he loved me." Your mind is not your own anymore. Things and folks don't get on your nerves at work. Traffic is at a standstill, and you're at peace. All you want to do is to get home, shower, and get dressed to see your love.

Love is wonderful, whether brand-new or time tested.

Has the party animal lost her bite?

"It's par-tee time!" Remember how that call to dance and meet men used to get your adrenaline pumping? No more, because the thrill is gone. The clubs are filled with twenty- and thirty-year-olds on the prowl. The music is so loud, it's impossible to talk if you do see someone interesting. Still, dance clubs are good places to meet men. You still love to dance, but if you do go, you'll just feel out of place. It's time to create a new social arena. Try this new twist on the old house party. I call it the BAM-JAM—"bring a man."

Call up ten of your girlfriends (each must work at a different company), and tell them you're throwing a singles party. Each is to bring one single, eligible man from her workplace or some other context (perhaps he is a successful entrepreneur). He is not her date; she should not be interested in him. But he should be a working, financially stable man. Have each friend provide a rundown of what her male friend does, how he looks, and what his interests are.

Next, invite the men. Let them know that ten interesting, attractive, single women are throwing a party and that they've been specially chosen to attend. Emphasize that there is no pressure, only a lot of fun, good food, and conversation. How can they refuse? They get to meet nine new women—and you get to meet nine new men.

Now, create a fun party atmosphere. The music should be just loud enough for dancing or talking. Have a table set up for cards, chess, checkers, or backgammon. Got a pool table? Great! Attire is smart–casual, so everyone is looking sharp. Good luck and have fun!

My party animal teeth are still sharp and I've still got that spark; I will take my party time to a higher, more creative, sophisticated level.

My last chapter remains to be written— a great romance novel?

"Can this be my life?" you ask yourself. All the chapters were coauthored by parents and you, teachers and you, husband and you, employers and you, children and you. Never just you.

What do you want to do with the rest of your life? Would you be thought of as crazy if you revealed that you're tired of being alone? Should you even want a romantic interlude at your age? The answer is yes. Give yourself permission to feel again.

You know you bring good stuff to a relationship. The first thing to do is to put your mind on romance. Think back to the preparations you used to make to go on a date. Start doing them now—hairdo, nails, clothes, all the preparations to bring out the warm, beautiful you. Even a trip to the supermarket or the mall can be reason enough to fix yourself up. You just never know. Men have to shop for food and clothes, too. And maybe, just maybe, you'll be closing your romantic story with, "And they lived happily ever after." You are a human treasure for a long–lasting relationship.

I am still writing the last chapters of my life, and there are plot twists and turns ahead as I want them.

Part Four

Inner Peace

groovin'

85   Inner peace for me.

86   I'll let the Divine be my director.

87   Letting go of old baggage lifts me up.

88   Family peace comes from an annually updated will and trust.

89   I'll spend heart-to-heart time with the Divine.

90   My mind is a powerful magnet that attracts only good to my life.

91   Before sleeping, I'll count my blessings.

92   I forgive myself and others, and I avoid anger and revenge.

93   I'm rich when my mind deposits good thoughts.

94   I can't change anyone else, so now peace abounds in me.

95   I live every day as though it's my last—and one day I'll be right.

96   The older I get, the more I let go and let God.

97   I'll live each day with passion, compassion, and love.

98   Because I know God, nothing can keep me down for long.

99   I accept change with an open heart and mind.

100 I'll send flowers and a card to an older friend—"just because."

101 When I am open to guidance from the Divine, my direction is clear.

102 Experience teaches that "this too shall pass."

103 As a child of God, I am heir to all life's riches.

104 I'll lighten my load by giving things away.

105 I look forward to the good that is yet to come.

106 During each day, I'll find time to relax in body and spirit.

107 More than ever, God is my help in every need.

108 When I need a quick refreshment, I take a prayer break.

109 I thank the Divine for unconditional love.

110 Mom and Dad are getting old.

111 Chew, digest, and grow by these ten sayings.

Living from
the inside out.

By the time you have reached forty-five, your recipe for a rich and satisfying spiritual life is probably as long as a Betty Crocker cookbook. Even if you never have baked or no longer bake, baking is a good metaphor for living from the inside out.

Think of your spiritual life as a cake, and you'll begin to see how your spirit has been seasoned by a teaspoon of this, a quarter cup of that, and a pinch of something else. Religion was probably the first ingredient that your parents stirred up in your soul. The challenging years of young adulthood came next, when you began to question your beliefs and maybe even forgo them or transform them. As you matured, you added philosophies, practices, and beliefs that were mixed into your sense of the world.

Those bland cups of white flour you sifted into your life's cake were the day-to-day routines you need to contend with—things such as tending to personal hygiene, tidying rooms, buying postage stamps, shopping for groceries, or stopping at a traffic signal. Flour is the stuff we do as life gets sifted out moment to moment. Because we do the things routinely, we don't need to spend too much time getting the lumps out.

We add milk to make the mixture pour easily. Examples of such liquefying life events are being appreciated for a deed well done, finding a movie or book that provides insight and hope, or getting a wonderful hug.

We add baking powder, but in small amounts. It leavens our lump, makes us pop up, opens our eyes. This baking powder is in the form of revelations and realizations: "I really goofed on that," or "I'll know not to do that again," or "I really was taken advantage of that time, but I'm wiser now." (To press my metaphor even harder: we often do not rise very high because we get too much of the flour of life, but not enough milk and sometimes even less insight. The baking powder encourages us to reach for the insight.)

So now, in the second half of life, it's time to add the spices and check the batter. The experiences of your lifetime have prompted you to reexamine your spirituality—its mixture of philosophies, practices, and beliefs. Instead of blindly following a pastor, priest, or rabbi, you've become a leader for yourself. You're the ultimate, unique blend of all that you have experienced and savored. How does it taste? If things are a little bland or flat, then you have time—this time—to bring your batter into balance. Meditate on the following affirmations, absorb them into your soul, and watch your own sweet spiritual cake rise.

Inner peace for me.

I picture the core of my body as fully functioning arteries and veins doing their God-given thing. At my solar plexus, my center, I see a stillness, a calm. I picture a very pale blue, almost white ball, no edges. It is free floating. It is free to bring its calming effect to any part of my body or spirit that needs rest.

If I'm anxious, the inner peace ball embraces the anxiety, and my tension is relieved. Just before I step on stage, I take three deep breaths and let the inner peace ball roll up and down my body. Now I'm ready to give my all. I consciously cultivate inner peace, the peace within.

What helps you find inner peace? For some women, it's the smell of baking cinnamon rolls, the warmth of a sun-drenched beach, the feeling of a warm bath or facial, the taste of a favorite beverage, the image of someone listening intently. Find that image or smell or feeling. Cultivate it. Savor it.

The next time that you are about to do something stressful, recall that entrance to your inner peace. If something else soothing comes to mind during this brief period, then focus on that and develop it.

I will find the pathway to my inner peace and tread it daily.

86

So you've gone to church, mosque, or temple for many years. Perhaps now you are a pillar in your religious community, or maybe you have not been inside a sanctuary for years.

I was raised an Episcopalian. As I matured and began to soul-search, I'd said the same prayers for too many years. I could say the response words automatically, and my mind would wander to things I had to do when church let out. I began to feel I didn't need such a formal structure to mediate between God and myself. So around age fifty, I stopped attending church. If you continue to find spiritual nurture in your place of worship, then I can only encourage you in your practice.

Since then, I have followed a daily plan. I pray just before I go to sleep by reading the next day's message in my Unity Daily Word. Every page is a surprise that seems to be written just for me.

Some people speak of God as the CEO—chief executive officer—in their lives. I prefer to speak about the Divine, who encourages my choices and creativity or draws forth from me more honest expressions—the Divine who, as behind a stage, is my director in the improvisation called life.

Whatever image or understanding sustains you, develop it and crystallize it in your thinking. How does it fit with your daily life? With your earlier experiences? What is there about this image or understanding that gives you comfort or consolation? Use aids for meditation or devotions or prayer. Keeping a journal can be helpful in this regard. Find what works for you and use it.

I will seek a spiritual practice that fits my needs and offers deeper meaning in my life.

87

Letting go of old baggage lifts me up.

When I first traveled, I packed so many changes of clothes—maybe it will be warm or cool, formal or informal—that I could hardly carry the suitcases. Some people lug so much hurt and anger with them wherever they go, I am amazed they can lift it all.

How heavy are your emotional suitcases? Unzip one of them, and examine the bricks and rocks and logs that make up the load. Perhaps someone provoked you to anger when you were a child. Perhaps in high school and into adulthood some disappointment festered into a large chip. Or maybe you haul a load of kindling wood that can be used as fuel for others to ignite.

Think of the wasted energy that has been used to carry this baggage. Or picture the constant frowns and contorted faces that are required to sustain the effort. Next time watch the face of someone struggling with a load or large package; over the years such frowns can become permanent. Age can bring on its own wrinkles, but why exacerbate the process? This load can also give you worries, and they can lead to ulcers, sickness, and other ugly pains. Let it go. Holding on won't hurt the other person. It hurts only you.

I will leave behind hurts and anger to make my load lighter.

Family peace comes from an annually updated will and trust.

Sometime in our forties, we take notice of our mortality. Perhaps it begins when our parents become aged or when we discover that we might not be able to fulfill all of our life's aspirations. For some this is so scary that they push it aside for a few more years. Others face it realistically and get their business in order. What does hearing the word "will" prompt in you?

Many think that wills are necessary only for the rich. Some think, I don't own any property or land, so what do I need a will for? Everyone needs a will because it is a good way to ensure enduring family peace.

Every family has a leader—not necessarily the eldest or male. In my family's case, I'm the youngest, and I'm the leader. Years ago, I called a reluctant family gathering. We are a close family, so my immediate family came, along with nieces, nephews, and cousins. We needed to meet because a family member had died, and the matters of the estate were not entirely clear. Well, I wanted to do this only once. I went around the room with the following questions (and, believe me, I kept notes and did follow up): (1) Is your will or trust current? (2) Where is it kept? (3) If a lawyer is holding it, then state the name and telephone number. (4) If it's at home, then state exactly where it is kept. (5) If papers are in a safe deposit box, whose name is authorized at the bank, and does he or she have a key? I insisted that family members who live alone must have one other name put on all accounts when no legal trust had been established.

I know that family members wanted to go home at that point, but we were only getting warmed up. We went on to personal articles, such as cars, televisions, heirlooms, jewelry. These items often cause more trouble than land inheritance. One diamond ring or grandfather clock can cause a generation's worth of infighting; sometimes the wounds go too deep to be healed.

In my family's case, it truly helped for everyone to witness other family members' wishes. It was important to know about the preference for a burial, funeral, cremation, or memorial. What and how; who wanted to donate organs, who wanted a living will (no machines to delay the inevitable). A will eliminates arguments and provides the basis for wishes to be carried out. All changes should be kept up-to-date and witnessed, and statements should be signed. New Year's Eve is my time to review and update my will or trust and make sure it expresses my desires.

I will establish a will and keep it current to reflect my changing wishes and situation.

I'll spend heart-to-heart time with the Divine.

A friend of mine once noted that many religious leaders like to direct our prayer time. "Whenever the minister says, 'Let us pray,'" she said, "he really means, 'Let me pray, and you listen.'" Her point is well taken. My concern comes from a different direction, however. Seldom do ministers address in prayer or announcements the day-to-day supports needed to help women in the second half of life. Then I look around; most religious gatherings have a large group of such women. (Spiritual leaders should help women find out about educational, cultural, leisure, and safety programs so that we can live enriched lives here and now.)

So what about prayer? Just waking up pain free, and having a close association with family and good friends—such a morning is a good reason to have a personal relationship with God. I find myself thanking God many times a day with many prayers, such as, "Thank you for a restful night," "Thank you for the great blue sky and fresh air at 6:00 a.m. when I walk," or, "Thank you for the parking space." As a very young teenager and to this day, there's a silent prayer that I say every time I hear an ambulance siren: "God bless whoever is suffering. Ease the pain and stop the bleeding. Make the heartbeat and breathing regular." I know God hears my prayer.

I call this spending heart-to-heart time with the Divine. Like my late-night meditations, it is both intentional and focused. Such a sense of gratitude also seems to focus my attention on what the Divine is doing next. What are the new gifts in life? Where are the new opportunities? How can I be of assistance to another?

I will seek the heart of the Divine in the new marvels of this world.

My mind is a powerful magnet that attracts only good to my life.

The little negative voice in your head will control you if you let it. "You know you can't do that." "Why do you let him get by with that?" "You know you shouldn't forgive her again." That little voice can be so nasty. When you were young, do you recall listening to that voice and acting upon its urgings? How often did it get you into trouble or put you on the defensive?

Time has taught me to turn down the volume knob or to talk back to that voice in a stern manner. The voice seems to be less powerful that way. "No, I'm not going to listen." "Be quiet. I know I can do it."

Denying your negative inner voice can become a good habit. I have found that my mind is like a magnet that attracts or picks different kinds of things. Focused in the negative voice direction, it can attract other negative thoughts, dredge up old hurts, nurse little demons. But focused in a positive voice direction—tuned in to the glory of God's world—it attracts other positive thoughts, surfaces joyous memories from long ago, and fosters kindnesses from others.

Turned in the negative direction, you can drown in a poisonous pit; turned in the positive direction, you can be lifted to a wondrous height where you are in control more and more. Your mind will begin automatically to censor negative thoughts. You'll attract other positive thinkers to be your associates, and life blossoms from an emptiness to a fullness.

An old saying that I've always lived by is, "You do good, you get good." Well, I also believe that if you think good, such good thoughts will multiply. You are at peace because your mind is free to be creative, free to think up ways to help others. Divine guidance is always at hand.

I know that my life is divinely guided.

Before sleeping, I'll count my blessings.

With each year, I find that I acquire more and more respect for life's simple pleasures. Mmm, doesn't that bed—your bed—feel good at the end of the day? The beds of others offer great variety. When you are a houseguest, the bed can range from a makeshift sofa in a corner to a beautiful, seldom-used bed in a guest room. (Just smell the mothballs.) Or while traveling, squeeze yourself into a narrow berth, on a train or a cruise ship, and let the rock-a-bye movement of the vessel lull you to sleep.

Regardless of the type of bed I'm sleeping in, the time when the house is quiet and the room is dark is the time when I relive my day. Was I fair and pleasant to those around me? Did I unconsciously hurt anyone? Did I pull my own load? Did I help a young person increase his or her self-esteem? What do I have to be thankful for? No aches or pains today. Family and friends are okay. Thank you, God!

I will always thank God for this day, ups and downs included.

92

I forgive myself and others, and I avoid anger and revenge.

Do you want peace, or do you insist on being right? The desire for revenge is a weakness of youth. They want to always be right. "He done me wrong" is one of the most popular revenge-causing statements, and it is often part-nered with anger in our younger lives. Revenge is also the cause of young children being torn between angry, divorced parents. "I'll make him pay by not letting him see his kids." How sad.

By middle age, you should be in control of your tem-per, at least to the point that you don't have to wield the big stick. After an angry episode, you're faced with how to deal with the person who received your anger. You should stretch your compassion and apologize if you are the one who erred, or even if you think you are due an apology and haven't received one. If the relationship is worth sav-ing, be secure enough to initiate the apology.

After the apology comes forgiveness. To forgive means to consciously wipe your slate clean. Don't be concerned whether the other person forgives you or not. That is not your business. But you must see the person you have wronged as a newborn, no negative baggage hanging on. You don't have to even the score. Only when the conflict has been resolved can you truly feel that your conscience is free enough of guilt to have your own peace.

I will forgive myself and others, and I will avoid anger and revenge.

I'm rich when my mind deposits good thoughts.

The minute you hear the word "rich," what comes to mind? Does it conjure up all the trappings that money can buy? Perhaps you think of things you'd love to buy and how happy you'd be with them. Maybe you think of being debt-free. A beautiful home to your own specifications, custom built, perhaps? How about a couple of homes in different parts of the world? While you're dreaming, you might as well throw in cars, a plane, and a boat. Don't forget a magnificent wardrobe with the finest fabrics and top designers. Now what? What else can you buy? You've got everything you ever wanted or thought you wanted.

But the joy is short-lived because you begin to lose sight of yourself in the midst of these possessions. You worked a lifetime for this dream, so what's wrong with this picture? Your money can't buy you a youthful body. Your money can't buy elastic blood vessels to lower your high blood pressure.

You begin to see that the things that you enjoy, really enjoy, are free to everyone. You couldn't see it earlier in your life. You begin to relive pleasant times in nature. The thoughts of a fully blossomed fruit tree, a butterfly in flight, a weed pushing up through a sidewalk crack—fun thoughts that will never leave you. Even when your dream of riches is gone, your mind is free to conjure a vision of the land of beauty where money is useless.

I will make deposits of good thoughts each day so that I will always have a rich store.

94

Who appointed you the chief overseer of your friends and mate? Why would you want that responsibility? Well, to be quite honest, you didn't set out to do it; it just happened because you saw a need and wanted to help. That your help was unsolicited didn't stop you. With good intentions, you forged ahead. If someone just wondered out loud, it was your cue to volunteer your wisdom. You took over the whole indecision and gave the person the strategy and the solution.

Certainly, some of this advice was wisely given and wisely accepted, and the end result was successful. Lucky you! But what about bad advice? Were you there to help pick up the pieces? Did you even know that your advice didn't work? Do others now walk, no run, in the other direction when your paths cross? Folks have to make their own decisions. Whether the decisions are good or bad, folks have to live their own lives. If your opinion is solicited, then give it, but always be sure to preface it by saying, "My opinion on this is...." The fallout of your new decision to give only solicited help is wonderful, blissful peace.

Many have been disappointed because they thought they could change someone for the better. People can change only themselves, if that is their desire, and then only with God's help. Speak with addicts recovering from drug, food, alcohol, or tobacco abuse, and they will tell you that they had to have God in their corner to be truly successful.

God frees me from the burden of trying to assume responsibility for the lives of other adults.

I live every day as though it's my last—and one day I'll be right.

One of the saddest things to hear another say is, "After the kids are out of school, we're going to take that trip," or "As soon as I get out of debt, I'm going to splurge on myself," or "We're sacrificing and putting a little something away for that rainy day, so we can't retire yet."

Who said tomorrow is promised to us? We're all here by God's grace. Life is made to be lived fully each day. Some persons are always putting their lives on hold. Once they achieve their financial goals, then something else is the excuse for their continued sacrificing. Who hasn't heard of persons who worked hard until retirement, only to die a couple of years later? Unfortunately, they never enjoyed living life fully day by day. View rainy days in the right perspective. Don't become so focused on "some day" mentality that you miss the "today" possibilities. "Give us this day."

I will live every day as though it's my last—and one day I'll be right.

96

The older I get, the more I let go and let God.

When you reached the second half of life, you probably thought you knew what was best for you, and in most instances, you were right.

Sometimes, however, we may not be good problem solvers because we mistakenly think we own the problems. We really believe that we have total responsibility for creating solutions, and this mind-set can be devastating. We think we know what to do, step by step, and set out to execute each phase. We end up frustrated and still clutching the problem.

To start the healing and really resolve the issue, we need to step back and let a divine solution begin. The first step has already happened: our personal path and trust have been challenged. But so has the second step: there is no place that God is not.

When I turn the problem over to divine guidance, I feel relief and peace. Experience has taught me that after I have done all that I can, I let divine guidance take over. It seems that all of my life I have seen myself in my desired plan, even down to how I'll look and feel. I may not have any of the ingredients that I will need to fulfill my plan, but God always provides. Divine timing brings together what is needed. The person drops by. The check comes in the mail. The phone rings. Always just in time. It has happened so often that I just plan, do what I can, and let it go—and let God.

I know God has good plans for me.

I'll live each day with passion, compassion, and love.

It is important to be responsive to others, to aim to be understanding and caring, but the conscience of another is not your responsibility. Experience has taught me that you've got to let people work out their own values and ideas. Your responsibility to other human beings is to be honest and understanding. Divine law will administer justice; meting out justice is not up to you. Just let it go.

Having passion on a day-to-day basis is having deep integrity for what you're about, whether it's sweeping the street or doing open-heart surgery. It's being committed to what you do, who you are. As you get older, your passion should grow, not fade. Shallowness disappeared with age because you've developed the courage to speak out. Loving others should be a given.

I love others because we as human beings are all expressions of God's love and grace.

98

Because I know God, nothing can keep me down for long.

In the first half of life, you had pluses. But did it ever seem that the pluses were plentiful enough? The drop from being on high was like being on a never-ending bungee drop. You tried to get a footing and a hand grip, but it was impossible. You kept bouncing up and down through all the problems.

You wondered why your older friends seemed to take life's problems in stride. They sort of faced things head-on, but they never seemed overly frustrated. Why? Because experience has proven that when they ask God to go with them and guide them, the road is made smooth. When I begin a job, I relax my body and mind to receive divine guidance and divine timing. I know God will put the right words in my mouth.

I face all tasks with confidence because God is my partner.

I accept change with an open heart and mind.

How many times have you heard someone say, "I'm in a groove, and it's great"? The person finally has stability and routine in life, but was he or she in danger of becoming stagnant? People get stuck. You see old friends who seem to be in a time warp. Have they grown at all? They still talk about the same old "Remember when" events of the past, even wear the same hairdos, now dyed red or black. Makeup the same, frozen in time.

I have learned that some change is necessary and stimulating. There is nothing to fear in change when you bring open-mindedness. Change is growth. Change is challenging. Your maturity makes you welcome change, not fear it. Over the years you have experienced too many changes to count and found them to be positive. God wants us to be able to accept change as part of the divine plan and part of our growth.

After I retired from dance, my career changed. I found that because I had been a teacher for twenty-eight years, having the skills of working with people of all ages was a plus in the field of advocacy for low-income families. I was an employment counselor for youth and a life skills counselor for homeless adults and women in nontraditional trades. Motivation and self-esteem skills were always prominent issues in my work as counselor, a carryover from my teaching days. I knew I would be successful in my career change because I love working with people, and God made the positions available to me.

I know that whatever changes I face, God is the director.

I'll send flowers and a card to an older friend— "just because."

The older you get, the more sensitive and watchful you become of seniors and their lifestyles. Unconsciously you're seeing yourself, saying, "I must remember to do thus and so, so that I won't go through what I see them experiencing." Some seniors' lives are very lonely. They live alone, and their friends have either moved away or died. Families have their own agendas. Offspring may give their mothers a hurried phone call, occasionally.

You can erase gloom and boredom from your life when you do kind things for others. Practicing goodwill gives your spirit a lift. Offer to do a difficult chore for a senior such as cleaning the stove or the refrigerator. Take her shopping or to the park. It could be the high point of her day. It tells her that she is not forgotten, that someone cares.

I can remember my mother's friend who lived alone. I saw her standing at a bus stop looking lost. I went back and picked her up and took her home. I went in with her and saw a half-eaten television dinner on the table. She was very frail. There was no one to look after her, and she was frightened of being alone. I asked her if she would like to move in with other women at a home. Tears came to her eyes, and she said yes. I found her a private home that housed three other older women. I knew the owner to be a kind person. It took a week to go through her things piece by piece, select what she couldn't do without, and move her. She finally felt safe. Her needs were tended to—meals, laundry, and company. I took her to her medical appointments. She lived happily for about two years longer. I feel honored to have served her.

I will find time to do an act of kindness for an elder or someone with a disability.

101

When I am open to guidance from the Divine, my direction is clear.

Thank you, God, for your guidance throughout my life. When you need guidance and direction, review the Twenty–third Psalm. "Be still and know that I am God." When your life experiences lead you to a fork in the road, you can be assured that God is near you to guide you to the correct path. When you're anxious, uncertain of what to do next, God's loving hand is there to hold you up, keep your head above water. Experience has taught you that God is always available to you; you can trust that God will see to it that things will work out right for you. At the time, you may have been disappointed because things didn't work out according to your plan, but if you don't turn your back on God, you'll see that divine guidance is always the right way.

God is there not only for major help, but for little things, too. I was in charge of the production of the first play that I wrote, *'Tis the Morning of My Life*. I had never produced a play before. I decided that because the family in the play was a contemporary, wealthy family, I needed lovely furniture, not the early Salvation Army that small theater productions usually use. God guided me to a furniture rental store. I bartered an ad in my program in exchange for a choice of any brand–new furniture I wanted. The set was beautiful and it contributed to our success. It opened the door for other theater groups to follow suit. It was God's doing.

God, make my direction clearer; open my eyes to your opportunities.

Experience teaches that "this too shall pass."

During your earlier years, you spent a lot of your time and emotional energy dealing with what you felt were earthshaking problems. First professional position, first baby, first parent's death, first time in overwhelming debt. It seems that you left problems at work only to be saturated with more of the same when you got home. You didn't feel your family members assumed their part of the load. You felt all decisions were yours. No suggestions or support from others. Your head was beginning to suffer. You couldn't sleep. You lost your appetite.

When you finally realized you couldn't be all-powerful—a superwoman—you turned to God in prayer. As soon as you confessed to yourself that you needed help, you were so relieved because the problem disappeared in time. You realize now that problems will arise from time to time. But now you know, having gone through many crises in your life, that the best thing to do is to ask for God's help, and all problems turn out to be temporary. They do pass.

I have faced major problems before, and I know that with God's presence, any new problems will also pass away.

103

As a child of God, I am heir to all life's riches.

You will receive according to your faith in the good things. Your wealth is your health, a richness that money cannot buy. A trusted friendship takes years to test and develop. You can't put a dollar value on a good, patient, loving family. The freedom to be yourself is a gift received after years of trial and error. You wonder what it would be like to suddenly find yourself a winner of the lottery millions. Money can buy only things. You know that now. Years ago you would have sold your soul to be a millionaire. No more. Now you know that the old saying "The best things in life are free" is true.

After my fifth back surgery, I was confined to a rehabilitation nursing facility for one month, April 1997, while I learned to walk again. The day that I was released was an amazing day. Not only was I glad to be starting my second phase of rehabilitation by being released, but I was glad to be going outside for the first time after a month indoors.

It was a sunny day. I remember thinking, "Gee, the sky is blue. Wow, look at how green that lawn is." Everything was extra bright and colorful. Everything looked new. The noises of the streets even sounded good. So take a good, deep breath and enjoy the beautiful sunrise.

I know that every sunrise is a gift from God.

I'll lighten my load by giving things away.

Remember when you bought that Tiffany lamp? You saved for months to get it. How proud you were to bring it home. Or the sculpture of a mother and child, beautiful in its warm, smooth ebony. The sets of china, silverware, linens that you no longer use. All of these things that you have lived with for decades are not important to you anymore. You don't even notice them when you enter the room.

The lightening of my load was serious business. I was a pioneer in my career, so I had many boxes of trophies, including two Dance Hall of Fame awards. I cleared my wall of citations and plaques. There was even a hand-thrown ceramic pot trophy. I saved my notes of choreography and lesson plans. I gathered up my original manuscripts for an autobiography, two cookbooks, three plays, and *Still Groovin'*. My acting career is documented on videos, including interviews and movies, all boxed and in the closet. It was a joy and relief to see the director of the African American Historical Museum and Oakland Library walk out of my home with boxes that housed part of my life, so to speak. I was equally happy to have more closet and shelf space freed up!

Invite a young person to your home, and give her the sculpture she has always admired. Call up your friend who loves your china and still entertains. Why should friends wait for your obituary? Let them enjoy your gifts now while you can enjoy their smiles. No one wants silver coffee and tea services anymore—too much trouble to keep polished. But churches and group homes would feel special owning it. You'll never forget the joy on their faces upon receiving your keepsakes. An added benefit of your giveaway is that you'll have fewer things to dust!

I'll lighten my load by giving things away—and watching others enjoy them now.

I look forward to the good that is yet to come.

Step by step, every day brings you closer to the good things that you seek and the good that is seeking you. Picture yourself standing under a waterfall, but instead of water, there are good things, bad things, not–too–good things, and not–too–bad things all showering down over you with equal intensity. All you have to do is to reach out and take what you want. The choice is yours. Bad and good stuff surround you, and sometimes you can't see the good for the bad. Other times, the front is good, and the bad is hiding but still attached to the good.

When you were younger, you simply stuck out a large net to catch whatever you could and as much as you could. But now your powers of discrimination and patience are getting more finely tuned. You're no longer out for as much as you can get. You want only the best. Now that you are centered on only the good, you can see through the bad to the good. Now life is peaceful.

I will reach out and take the good that God offers me.

106

During each day, I'll find time to relax in body and spirit.

Did it really take more than forty years to learn that I am not made of iron? Yes, it did. Before that, I thought I was invincible. I was the first to arrive and the last to leave. If I'm due at work at 8:00 a.m., I'm there at 7:30. I don't like to hit the ground running. I like to get where I'm going and have time to segue from personal to professional life. I call it "having my moment." By being early, I have time to relax my body and mind and start my activity from a centered place.

My work style was also aggressive. "Get ahead" was my tune. I didn't realize that the more work I took on, the more my associates were willing to step back and let me wear myself out. I wondered how folks found the time to hang out by the water cooler and the coffee room several times a day. There's an old saying that goes, "If you put your hand in a bucket of water, splashed it around, and caused waves, everyone paid attention to you. But when you took your hand out of the bucket of water, it became calm and still, and no one knew your hand had even been there." I have learned that no one is indispensable—and that anyone can make a splash.

Now you ask yourself how to find the time in your busy schedule. Take your appointment book, and block out some time. Put down "Meet with self." Schedule yourself into a personal meeting to chill out. Go to a movie; stay in bed; drive to a park. Just don't do anything demanding.

Now I have finally learned to pace myself. I plan downtime for myself. Nowadays "chill out" is my tune.

More than ever,
God is my help in every need.

"God is my help in every need" is a line from Unity's prayer of faith. The prayer was my family's table grace we said in unison at each meal. Maybe when you were younger, you went to church and prayed, but you hadn't learned the total lesson of accepting the best for yourself. You settled for second best all too often because you were not able to achieve all you desired by yourself or with the limited assistance at your disposal. You had not learned to take God as your resource in every facet of your life. You felt you could go it alone in your work. Now you know better who the real Professional is and from whom your knowledge comes. Only by God's grace are you considered a professional.

Sometimes I just have to stop in awe and thank God. Where did all the blessings come from? As I meditate on God's goodness, it's as if I'm observing choreography unfold. Poems come to me so quickly that I can hardly write them down fast enough. I enjoy writing personalized poems to loved ones, but where do the words come from, and so fast? Whole dance suites would spill out of my mind when needed.

Creative ideas on a range of subjects just come to me. Amazing grace. God can solve all problems or troublesome situations; all you have to do is to ask for guidance.

I know that there is no place that God is not.

108

When I need a quick refreshment,
I take a prayer break.

I find that many times throughout the day I need prayer breaks, regardless of where I am or what I'm doing. I don't need to have silence or to be alone to say a prayer. I just take a deep breath and go inside myself. My prayers of "Thank you, God!" give me the needed boost. Or if things aren't going well, I remember to release all problems into God's care. As soon as I do this, it's as if a cloud lifts from me, and I can see clearly. I don't even have to go into the details. God knows. Just say, "It's yours, God. Guide me." You'll know that your next course of action will be absolutely correct because it is divinely given to you. You are calm and ready to face the world with a new attitude.

If you were to peek at my daily appointment book, you would see the letters "TYG" (Thank you, God) throughout. TYG goes after each event that needed a blessing or surprise blessing, like an unexpected treat. If an activity has been successfully completed, I put TYG beside it. Completion of this book. A wonderful night on the town. A surprise phone call from a friend. Paydays. A Chinese meal. And on and on and on.

Get started now. Learn the lesson of saying, "I let go. It's yours, God." It will ease you into your latter years with indescribable joy and peace.

I thank the Divine for unconditional love.

There is no excuse for doubting yourself. You spent your earlier years doing that. When things flow easily, you're on the right track. Things that are difficult to perceive or work through are usually wrong for you. God is always trying to make your way smooth, but you don't accept the divine offerings, so you forge ahead. Thank goodness, God doesn't give up when you don't accept divine guidance! Only when you can truly believe that God wants good for you and you give your burdens to God's intelligence does your life have the joy and peace you seek. You know that God is always there for you through thick and thin. Through doubt and faith, God is always steady.

A song's lyrics say, "If it don't fit, don't force it." Well, some of us are forever trying to force some aspect of our lives that doesn't fit into God's plan for us. All it does is delay the fulfillment of our good.

I remember a get-rich-quick scheme that swept the town. Everyone was investing. We all had the bonus money spent in advance. It sounded so good. Too good. I actually saw folks with a lot of money. I felt trepidation and discomfort, but I didn't honor those feelings. God was trying to make me see that the scheme didn't fit. We all lost some money. Thank goodness my losses were small. Some got in and out before us...a lesson learned.

I know that God's support is steady.

110

Your mother is sixty-eight, and your father is seventy. You never thought the term "senior citizens" would apply to your vital parents. But lately you are noticing definite changes, especially with your father. It used to be that he couldn't wait to get out on the tennis courts. Now he doesn't even want to hit a few balls with you. He is content to watch tennis on TV. He is still involved in church activities, but he doesn't politick to be elected to any offices anymore. He always loved the challenge of campaigning, and he always won. Now, when you drop by during the daytime, he is often in his lounge chair, napping. His trips to the doctor seem to be more frequent. Nothing serious—just a little more pain here and there.

Your mother's changes are more subtle. Women are lucky because men age faster than women, or at least that's what we choose to believe. Your mother still wants to go out, but since your father doesn't want to, she stays home, too. Her friends are in the same boat, so the camaraderie of friendships is slipping away. Her active grandmother role that she loved has changed. No more little toys to shop for or ice cream cones to enjoy. The kids don't spend the night anymore. They visit. It's adult to adult or teens now. She goes to the community center some days and enjoys the classes. Her favorite is line dancing. Yes, line dancing. But your father won't go. He says he doesn't want to be around those "old geezers." They eat out more often at those early–bird dinner places because she doesn't feel like cooking all the time.

You're beginning to see the writing on the wall, and it's scary. What's going to happen when she can't cook, or he can't drive himself to the doctor? What will be the impact on your life and your family? Know now that the impact will be enormous. You're lucky if they'll discuss anticipated problems with you. Oftentimes, they won't talk about it.

For your peace of mind, make a what–if list of possible problems and how you would solve them. You must have a plan, even if you do not share it with them, because one day your role may change. You may become their parent.

I will bring peace to my life by preparing for my parents' aging.

111

Chew, digest, and grow by these ten sayings.

Who said them? I don't know. I've just heard some of them over the years and think they're great. Some I invented.

1. When you're casual about life, you'll end up a casualty.
2. Every accomplishment starts with the decision to try.
3. What great achievement has been performed by the person who told you it couldn't be done?
4. If you stand for nothing, you'll fall for anything.
5. If you aim at nothing, you'll hit it every time.
6. If something knocks you down, try to land on your back 'cause if you can look up, you can get up.
7. You can't soar like an eagle if you're running around with pigeons.
8. Yesterday is history. Tomorrow is a mystery. Today is a gift. That's why it's called the present.
9. If you like what you've been getting, keep doing what you've been doing.
10. Periodic self-pampering is profitable.

I can lift my spirit by using any of these affirmations in the second half of my life.

About the Author

Ruth Beckford toured professionally with the Katherine Dunham African Caribbean Dance Company at age 17 and was the first black student at the Anna Halprin/Welland Lathrop Dance Studio in San Francisco. She founded and directed the first city-funded recreational dance program in Oakland, worked with the Oakland Ensemble Theatre and has written or co-written three plays, as well as a biography of Katherine Dunham.